Wisdom Chi Kung

Wisdom
Chi Kung

Practices for Enlivening
the Brain with Chi Energy

Mantak Chia

Destiny Books
Rochester, Vermont

Destiny Books
One Park Street
Rochester, Vermont 05767
www.DestinyBooks.com

Destiny Books is a division of Inner Traditions International

Library of Congress Cataloging-in-Publication Data
Chia, Mantak, 1944–
  Wisdom chi kung : practices for enlivening the brain with chi energy / Mantak Chia.
    p. cm.
  Originally published under title: Wisdom chi kung : opening the brain to wisdom. Thailand : Universal Tao Publications, 2005.
  Includes bibliographical references and index.
  ISBN: 978-1-59477-136-1 (pbk.)
  1. Qi gong. 2. Hygiene, Taoist. I. Title.
  RA781.8 .C473 2008
  613.7/1489 22
                                                              2008009988
Printed and bound in China by Regent Publishing

10 9 8 7 6 5 4 3 2 1

Text design and layout by Jon Desautels
This book was typeset in Jansen with Present used as the display typeface

Contents

Acknowledgments

The Universal Tao Publications staff involved in the preparation and production of *Wisdom Chi Kung: Practices for Enlivening the Brain with Chi Energy* extend our gratitude to the many generations of Taoist masters who have passed on their special lineage as an unbroken oral transmission over thousands of years. We wish to thank the thousands of unknown men and women of the Chinese healing arts who developed many of the techniques and concepts presented in this book.

We wish to thank Taoist Master Yi Eng who worked so patiently to teach his students for his openness in transmitting the formulas of Taoist Inner Alchemy.

We offer our eternal gratitude to our parents and teachers for their many gifts to us. Remembering them brings joy and satisfaction to our continued efforts in presenting the Universal Tao System. As always, their contribution has been crucial in presenting the concepts and techniques of the Universal Tao.

We thank the many contributors essential to this book's final form: The editorial and production staff at Inner Traditions/Destiny Books for their efforts to clarify the text and produce a handsome new edition of the book, Victoria Sant'Ambrogio for her line edit of the new edition, and the artist, Juan Li, for his fine illustrations; as always, he has played an integral role in presenting the Universal Tao concepts and techniques.

We wish to thank the following people who contributed to the earlier editions of this book: Angela Dawn Babcock for her writing and editorial contributions; Udon for his illustrations, book layout, and beautiful cover; James O'Connell and Jean Chilton for their assistance in preparing, editing, and proofreading the manuscript; Jettaya Phaobtong and Saumya Comer for their editorial contributions to the earlier revised edition of this book; and our Thai Production team, Raruen Keawpadung, Saysunee Yongyod, Udon Jandee, and Saniem Chaisarn.

Putting Wisdom Chi Kung into Practice

The practices described in this book have been used successfully for thousands of years by Taoists trained by personal instruction. Readers should not undertake the practice without receiving personal transmission and training from a certified instructor of the Universal Tao, since certain of these practices, if done improperly, may cause injury or result in health problems. This book is intended to supplement individual training by the Universal Tao and to serve as a reference guide for these practices. Anyone who undertakes these practices on the basis of this book alone, does so entirely at his or her own risk.

The meditations, practices, and techniques described herein are *not* intended to be used as an alternative to or substitute for professional medical treatment and care. If any readers are suffering from illnesses based on mental or emotional disorders, an appropriate professional health care practitioner or therapist should be consulted. Such problems should be corrected before you start training.

This book does not attempt to give any medical diagnosis, treatment, prescription, or remedial recommendation in relation to any human disease, ailment, suffering, or physical condition whatsoever.

Neither the Universal Tao nor its staff and instructors can be responsible for the consequences of any practice or misuse of the information contained in this book. If the reader undertakes any exercise without strictly following the instructions, notes, and warnings, the responsibility must lie solely with the reader.

Western Science Meets the Tao

RESEARCH ON THE TAO

The material presented in this book is a condensation of the knowledge and experience gained from thirty years of teaching. Over these years, I have been able to devise a very simple and effective way of gaining awareness of the mind, body, and emotions, through a series of meditations (fig. 1.1). In recent times, Western researchers have been studying

You just need to learn some simple practices that will help your brain give up its unnecessary and unproductive hold on many of your conscious, intuitive, and emotional experiences.

Fig. 1.1. Empty the mind down to the tan tien.

the effects of these meditations, using the latest, most sophisticated technologies to measure brain waves and energy levels. As a result, research has recently "proven" these meditations to be among the most effective forms of quieting the mind and energizing the body with chi (or qi).

Many research groups have investigated the methods and practices that we teach in the Universal Tao. More and more scientists have discovered, using these bio-electro-measurement techniques, that the details of the ancient Taoist forms coincide with their conceptual theories. But these scientists bypass a complete understanding of the connection of the wisdom of the body and mind. The understanding of these concepts is the "link" of information that we will expand upon in the upcoming chapters of *Wisdom Chi Kung*.

Research has also been done on many monks and practitioners of other kinds of meditation than the ones we present to you in this book. This research has found that through various techniques, in a very deep meditation, practitioners can virtually stop their brain waves. However, in this state, the alpha and theta brain waves that cycle healing energy in the physical body are not present. Healing energy is a vibrational frequency that "charges" our system with its potential highest charge to increase the functioning of the body.

So the potential of a clear mind, or a meditative state, is present when the brain waves are stopped. Yet healing energy, which is one of the main focuses of Taoist meditation, is not present at all (fig. 1.2).

In 1996, I was invited to Vienna to participate in a scientific study using modern measurement techniques. Chapter 3 describes this study in more detail. To start, I was able to help the researchers verify the results of previous studies of the brain in a meditative state. But using Taoist practices, I was then also able to increase the measurable brain waves in a surprising manner. The meaning of this kind of testing was still not very clear. I myself really didn't understand how I was creating these results. Basically, I was performing two practices: The first was the Inner Smile (fig. 1.3). The second was working with orgasmic energy to raise chi and energize the brain—Wisdom Chi Kung.

Fig. 1.2. Many forms of meditation do not
produce healing energy.

Fig. 1.3. The Inner Smile meditation: healing
energy is present.

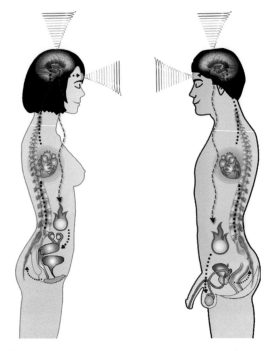

Fig. 1.4. Sexual energy synchronizes the left and right brain.

When focusing on these energies, the frequency heightens and the beta, alpha, and theta waves all rise up to a very high level, at which the left and right brains synchronize (fig. 1.4). Normally it would be assumed impossible for all three brain waves to be at a high level at the same time. It would be similar to a person driving a car while asleep.

But as we explain step by step in this book, the meditations actually increase consciousness and awareness by completely activating the physical body's energetic potentials.

BUDDHA, ZEN, AND THE TAO

As part of my continued research in Vienna, I became familiar with the chi machine, which measures "ultraslow brainwave potentials" (fig. 1.5). The scientists there had also been researching this material for some time and had extensive information on the outcomes of medita-

Ultraslow brain-wave potentials are measured while in Vienna.

Fig. 1.5. Taoist meditation increases physical energy.

tion by Buddhist monks and Zen masters. With the chi machine they had amassed evidence similar to the points already mentioned, the most interesting information being that with these forms of meditation, the practitioner was creating no new energy in the body and was actually depleting the body of its vital force.

Brain activity determines how much energy we have, and if we do not do something with the energy in the brain, then our energy is lost.

The researchers discovered that the brain-energy level of people during normal activity was about sixty units. This means that if you rest well and get up ready for the day, your brain energy should be at this level. If you start at this normal level and proceed through your everyday activities—walking, sitting, thinking, talking—at the end of the day your energy level may have gone down to ten or even just five units. At that level, you have no energy to keep working and you have to rest. So, the researchers concluded, if we could find a way to increase the level of energy in the brain to one hundred or two hundred units, we would have so much more energy to carry out our daily activities.

This is exactly what the Taoist meditation practices accomplish (see figs. 1.6, 1.7, and 1.8 on pages 6 and 7). And, in fact, many of the other meditation techniques originally had this purpose as well. It would seem that this kind of practice would be very useful for people who want to continue to have their place in the world.

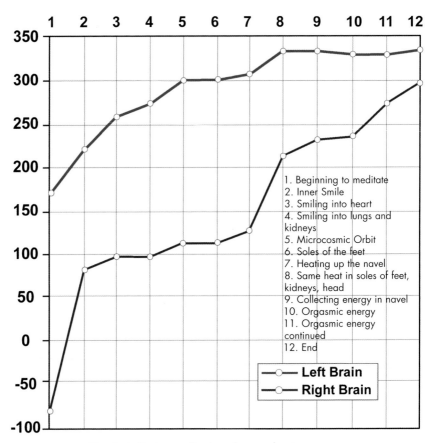

Fig. 1.6. Taoist meditation charges brain energy.

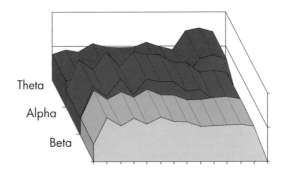

Fig. 1.7. Alpha and theta waves increase
during the Inner Smile meditation.

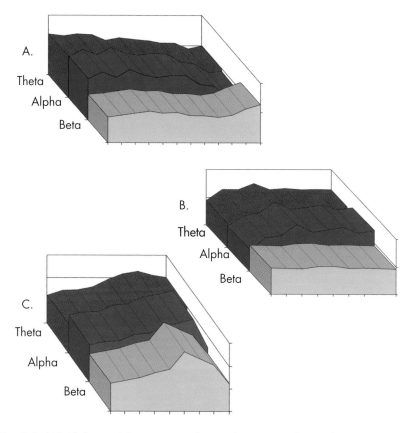

Fig. 1.8. (A) Alpha and theta waves alter in dominance during the Microcosmic Orbit meditation. (B) The Cosmic Healing Sounds meditation results in increases in alpha and theta frequencies. There are minimal beta brain waves; the brain reaches a state of stillness and internal focus. (C) Orgasmic Upward Draw increases the alpha and theta levels.

The other forms of meditation, where all brain-wave activity stops, are fine if you want to live in a cave or a convent or a temple. You can sit there, so full of bliss, so content, with little energy in the body, and with no concern that when you come out of your meditation, you have no energy for going back out into the world. These meditations in which people are sitting down, stopping their brain waves, and raising some energy up into the brain, are just not sufficient because when the meditation ends, the energy does not hold. This is not what most of us are looking for. This sort of meditation is like trying to charge your battery when it will not hold a charge. That is not the way.

So, for those people who wish to remove themselves from the world, the Buddhist and Zen methods of meditation serve a purpose. Just empty the mind into the universe and that's it, forget everything, leave nothing in the body. But for the rest of the six and a half billion people on the earth, I don't think we can do that. Too many people are too disconnected from their bodies already; the last thing most people need to do is give their energy away to the universe.

CULTIVATE YOUR UNIVERSAL CHI THROUGH THE TAO

The Taoists say, cultivate this chi from the universe, for the sake of both wisdom and energy (fig. 1.9). If we're here on this planet, why not have as much energy as humanly possible?

Fig. 1.9. Many forms of meditation may disconnect you from the outside world, whereas Taoist forms will connect you with the universe.

What we are looking for is for the physical energy to rise up, and when we stop meditation, for the energy to continue to rise up and charge into the brain. When we do the Inner Smile, the energy rises into the brain, and the energy that develops in ten minutes during this time stays in the body for up to eight hours.

When you work with the arousal orgasm energy, the energy charges up into the brain and the left and right brains synchronize. When you end the practice, the energy continues to rise into the brain. If you do this practice for fifteen minutes and direct the energy into each organ, then your ability to plan and organize your daily life is greatly enhanced.

THE GUT BRAIN AND THE TAO

The Taoists believe that when we experience a strong emotion, it is stored and recalled by the organs. Taoists know that these experiences cannot be erased. That is why powerful negative experiences in childhood later become the source or foundation of psychological problems. Many psychologists spend a lot of time trying to reach these experiences, which are locked away in the organs.

This is very much in accordance with the recent findings in the scientific community on the "gut brain"—by definition, the brain in the gut. There is much ongoing research into whether this gut brain can actually think and correspond with the head brain (see chapter 2). Can it send and receive impulses, experience and respond to emotions? Do organs have the ability to make decisions?

Taoists say yes, the gut brain can think. I am going to show you in upcoming chapters that this is true: the gut brain and the organs can think.

Wisdom Chi Kung Theory

Western science has discovered that when people are heavy thinkers, when they worry a lot, when their thoughts dwell on anger, jealousy, hatred, or other negative emotions, their brain activity can consume 80 percent of all their total body energy. The brain is a heavy user of energy and when it begins to use its energy, it doesn't stop unless it is told to. The rest of the body is left with only 20 percent of the energy to use for all the other intricate functions needed for daily activity. It's not hard to imagine why, at the end of the day, most people go home and "veg out" in front of the television. There is not enough energy left in the body to do anything.

One of the things that many religions have tried to do through meditation is to figure out how to stop people from thinking. How do you stop the monkey mind from its constant spinning? All this activity does not even stop at the end of the day but continues on into the night during dreaming. In this chapter, we will introduce you to the concept of monkey mind and how to recognize it when it begins. In later chapters you will learn how to respond correctly to its perpetual activity.

BASIS OF THEORY

To begin with, the whole secret of the practice is simply this: just smile down, relax, and picture the eyes like sunlight shining on the water; suddenly you will start to feel something like steam beginning to rise up from your sacrum. You will feel this energy move up and begin to charge the brain. Now, if you expand the mind out and connect with the universe, then bring the energy back and store it in the organs, when that energy is transformed and charged back up to the brain, it will bring the brain functioning to a new level. This energy has been transformed and digested so that the brain can use it effectively. This is very different from storing universal energy in the brain itself. The effort to store undigested universal energy in the brain can actually produce something like an allergic reaction, a kind of "energy indigestion." The brain can have a very strong reaction to this unprocessed energy.

In the Taoist practices, we are always concerned about the lower tan tien (fig. 2.1). The energy in the lower tan tien is the basis of all the higher practices. Wherever your mind goes, the chi will go; that is

Fig. 2.1. Smile down and fill the tan tien with chi.

where the fire will be burning. So you must always keep your mind on the lower tan tien, or else this fire will burn out. When the fire burns out, the body loses an immense amount of life force. If this happens, the mind then needs to be turned in, after which it can expand out. We will explore this topic further in later chapters.

INTRODUCTION TO MONKEY MIND

In the West, the common belief is that the brain, the vital organs, the sexual organs, and the energy of the body are all separate. Compounding this mistaken belief, religions make out the sexual function to be sinful. But it should be obvious that it is impossible to suppress the natural instinct to have sex. The problem is that sex has become a very basic drain on everyone, because we approach it in the wrong way. So how do we manage this energy and maintain it?

The sexual energy and the brain energy are the same energy, and their communication with each other is vital for healthy functioning. The obstacle to this communication arises from the fact that our mind is patterned to function continuously without receiving messages or impulses from the rest of the body. The mind will spin, voluntarily and involuntarily, with no direction, simply for the purpose of maintaining itself. With no structure or discipline, this monkey mind will run loose and rampant. In the upcoming chapters, we describe in detail how to begin to manage this monkey mind and connect it down to our sexual organs, turning this generated energy into fuel for the body (fig. 2.2).

THE INNER SMILE

The most essential point is to connect all the organs and the brain. So, you might ask, how am I going to make this connection? And I say, it is nothing more than a smile (fig. 2.3). Nothing more. It took me thirty years to understand this. Even then, it wasn't until all the testing was done that it all became clear.

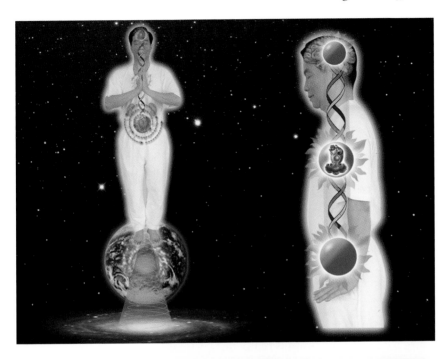

Fig. 2.2. Connecting
the energies

Fig. 2.3. Inner Smile
into the organs

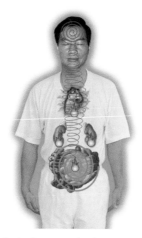

Fig. 2.4. Connect the brain and the
organs to filter the energy.

Our whole goal is to increase the capacity of the brain to hold energy, because the brain is really not very capable of "holding energy." The brain can easily overheat, actually "cooking" the brain. When the brain gets too cooked, there can be detrimental experiences, such as psychological damage. Many people have experienced too much heat in the brain and ended up in the hospital because their heightened experiences brought too much undigested brain food, turning it into sickness rather than nutrition. Smiling into the organs will allow us to filter energy, giving just enough to charge the brain and revitalize the organs (fig. 2.4).

THE SECOND BRAIN

In 1996, the *New York Times* published the article, "Complex and Hidden Brain in the Gut Makes Stomachaches and Butterflies." The entire article is dedicated to explaining to the public how "the gut has a mind of its own, known as the enteric nervous system, located in sheaths of tissue lining the esophagus, stomach, small intestine, and colon." Because of its direct relevance to the material we present in this book, this section will quote heavily from the article. The authors explain that the gut brain is "a network of neurons, neurotransmitters, and proteins that zap messages between neurons and support cells like those found in the brain, and a complex circuitry enables it to act independently to send and receive impulses, record experiences, and respond to emotions." Nearly every substance that helps run and control the brain has also been found in the gut.

"Since offspring need to eat and digest food at birth, nature seems to have preserved the enteric nervous system as an independent circuit only loosely connected to the central nervous system. A clump of tissue called the neural crest forms early in embryogenesis; one section turns into the central nervous system, another piece migrates to become the enteric nervous system. Only later are the two nervous systems connected via a cable called the vagus nerve" (figs. 2.5 and 2.6).

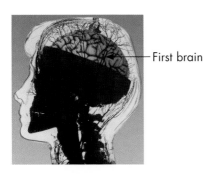
First brain

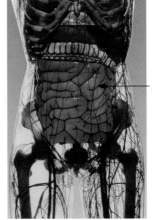
Second brain

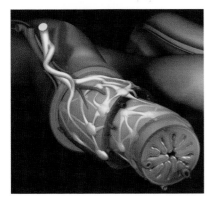
Cross-section
of the neurons
in the large
intestine

Fig. 2.5. The enteric nervous system feeds
the second brain.

Brain

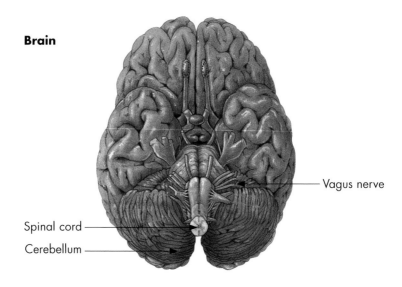

Vagus nerve

Spinal cord

Cerebellum

Organs

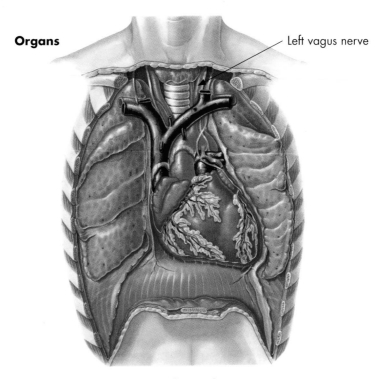

Left vagus nerve

Fig. 2.6. Enteric and central nervous systems
connected by vagus nerve

"The gut contains 100 million neurons—more than the spinal cord has. Yet the vagus nerve only sends a couple of thousand nerve fibers to the gut (fig. 2.7). The brain sends signals to the gut by talking to a small number of 'command neurons,' which in turn send signals to gut interneurons that carry messages up and down the pipe. Both kinds of neurons are spread throughout two layers of gut tissue called the myenteric plexus and the submuscosal plexus."

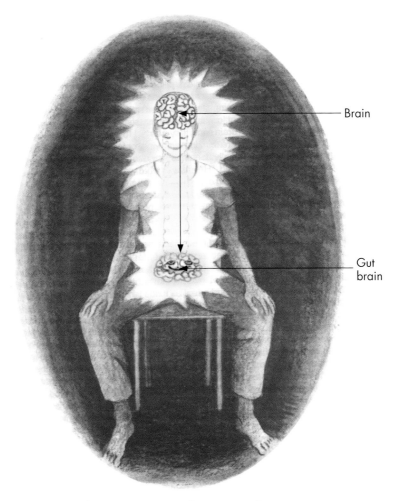

Fig. 2.7. The vagus nerve sends corresponding messages
to the gut brain.

"The gut's brain and the head's brain act the same way when they are deprived of input from the outside world. During sleep, the head's brain produces 90-minute cycles of slow-wave sleep punctuated by periods of rapid-eye-movement sleep, in which dreams occur (fig. 2.8). During the night, when it has no food, the gut's brain produces 90-minute cycles of slow-wave muscle contractions punctuated by short bursts of rapid muscle movements. Such cross talk also explains many drug interactions; psychic drugs that affect the brain are very likely to have an effect on the gut as well." The gut can think.

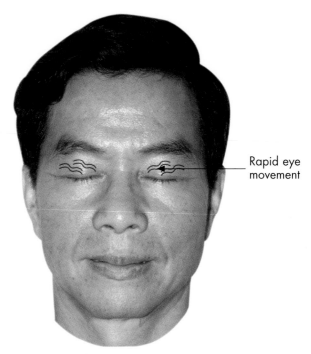

Rapid eye movement

Fig. 2.8. Rapid eye movement during sleep

For centuries, Taoists have known about this complex and hidden brain in the gut. They have understood and worked with the specific alchemy of the body, and used its simplicity for healing purposes.

TRANSFORMATION CYCLES

We can gain understanding of our human life by reflecting on the natural cycles we see around us. For example, if we consider water and its properties, we can find a reflection of the cycles of human life. The human body is about 90 percent water. Starting with its most rigid state, ice, the ice changes to liquid water, and then the liquid changes to steam or vapor (fig. 2.9).

Ice   Water   Steam

Fig. 2.9. Transformation cycle: ice, liquid, and steam

This transformation is occurring every day when the sun shines on the water. Without the sun shining on the water, very quickly everything that we know of on Earth would vanish. Without the vapor, there would be no rain. We've had the same water going around in this recycled manner for a hundred million years. The ancient Taoists said that the secret of immortality is to transform all liquids into life force.

RECONNECTING MIND, BODY, SPIRIT

Taoism believes that the mind, body, and spirit must work together in the process of generating and storing energy.

1. The sexual organs: The Taoists discovered that although the sexual organs are responsible for *generating* life-force energy, they cannot store the energy efficiently. Once a certain amount of energy has been generated, some energy has to be released.

2. The brain: The brain can access and generate the higher forces, but again, it is not easy to store this energy in the brain. We need to train the brain to increase its ability and its capacity to store energy. The brain energy, when increased to a certain level, can enable more synapses to grow, and can help convert protein into material the brain cells can use. Taoists believe that with training and practice, we can learn to grow more brain and nerve cells, as well as increase the number of synapses or connections between the nerve cells in the central nervous system.

3. The other organs: The organs of the body can also generate energy, but much less than the sexual organs and the brain. They do, however, have a much greater capacity to store and transform energy.

4. The three tan tiens: The three tan tiens can also store energy as well as transform and supply it to the brain, spinal cord, sexual organs, and other organs.

The aim of the basic Taoist training is to integrate the brain, sexual organs, and internal organs into one system. If the brain generates an excess of energy, the body can store this energy in the organs. The body can also store excess sexual energy in the organs and the three tan tiens. If, in the course of our practice, the brain generates a surplus of the higher-force energy and we are unable to store this energy, we end up having to throw it away. This is like preparing food for one hundred people, and allowing only one person to eat. The rest is wasted. Likewise, when we produce too much sexual energy and we have no practice in how to store it, the energy will be wasted.

Now consider this: even if your brain energy is connected with your sexual energy and this energy rises up into the brain, if you do not have the connection established with the organs, all this energy has no place to be stored. If there is no connection between the brain and the organs, there is no way to store the energy; if you have a lot of energy in the brain, the brain has no alternative but to dump it out. Once you have made the connection between the organs and the brain, when there is excess energy in the brain you just dump it down into the organs and store it there; the organs can store and transform it. Any energy that is excess, the organs can store and transform back into useful energy (fig. 2.10).

The simple formula is the same one that has been used in the Tao for five thousand years. Empty the mind to the tan tien and fill the tan tien with chi. When you empty the mind to the tan tien, 80 percent of the energy in the brain is returned to the organs, and you have this

Fig. 2.10. Releasing excess energy from brain to organs

80 percent of the energy available to use. The organs will absorb and store the energy, transform it, and return it to the brain in a useful form. When the brain is emptied, it is then ready to be filled by the energy returning to it from the organs. When that transformed energy rises back up and charges into the brain, the memory and functioning of the brain is improved (fig. 2.11).

The more you empty the brain to the tan tien and the more that energy is transformed and charged back to the brain, the fewer problems you will have.

You simply learn to smile down, you learn to relax, to let go, to empty the mind. It is as if you are pulling a plug, and the water just flows down, down to the abdomen—and that's it: the brain empties.

Fig. 2.11. Transformed energy will improve mental functioning.

INCREASE SEXUAL FUNCTION

Now, concerning the sexual organs, in the male, the prostate gland actually generates the most energy. Be aware of the prostate gland and lightly contract it; this will release tremendous energy during the male orgasm when the prostate gland is contracting and pulsing.

The testicles also have a lot of energy. This energy is waiting for activation; we can call this sexual desire (fig. 2.12).

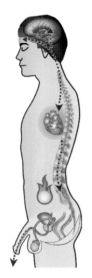

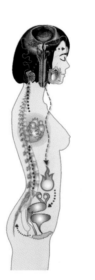

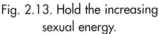

Fig. 2.12. Sexual activation increases desire.

Fig. 2.13. Hold the increasing sexual energy.

When arousal occurs, the energy rises up and is available to use. But normally, we do not know how to hold this energy. It immediately leaks out through the eyes or the voice, or through sexual activity. When we learn how to smile, first to the vital organs, then to the sexual organs, and we are aware of the brain and the organs, the sexual energy rises upward (fig. 2.13). It's really quite simple, but when you do not understand the connection, there is no way to maintain and hold this energy. The sexual organs give us most of our vital, creative, life-force energy.

Just look at modern advertising (fig. 2.14). Sex sells! Advertisers associate their product with sexual arousal so that when you feel excitement, you will have the image of their product flashing in your mind; sexual temptation, sexual desire, becomes the desire for their product. Everywhere you go there is sexual stimuli, because the sexual organs produce immense energy. The Tao texts say, "Return the sexual energy to recharge, revitalize and rejuvenate the brain."

Fig. 2.14. Sexual innuendos in advertising

A man is easy to arouse, because the sperm have a tail. When there is no arousal, the sperm stay in an inactive state in the testicles. When they see something that is very beautiful and causes arousal, the tail of each of those millions of sperm starts vibrating. The tail begins vibrating at over two thousand times per second. Very, very quickly! When the tail is vibrating at that frequency, it begins to generate the male sexual drive; this we call Jing Chi (or Ching Chi), sexual energy (fig. 2.15). Just imagine: a healthy man produces about 200 to 500 million sperm, and when they are all vibrating at the same time . . .

The woman is much slower to arouse. When the woman is aroused, the tiny hairs in the vaginal canal are vibrating very quickly. This too is the Jing Chi (fig. 2.16). The sexual glands release hormones, thus there is a chemical response as well as an energy response arising from the rapidly vibrating hairs in the vaginal canal. After the length of time it takes the woman to reach maximum pleasure, her sexual organs soften and release fluid. This fluid is what continually lubricates the

Fig. 2.15. Cultivating male Jing Chi

Fig. 2.16. Cultivating female Jing Chi

vagina, keeping her moist during intercourse. If this lubrication is not flowing, often the woman has broken off her emotional connection with the man, and sex is no longer pleasurable. So you can imagine: if a woman really does not "love" the man, pleasurable sex will be tough to come by.

FUSION PRACTICE

For those of you who have taken the Fusion practice, you know that when you first learn this practice it can seem very confusing (fig. 2.17). In this practice we learn to train the mind to keep track of and focus on up to twenty objects at the same time. The mind must be very clear. Every different kind of energy has to be traced individually. When your brain energy starts to increase its balance, you can do fifteen or twenty things at the same time with focus and clarity.

Fig. 2.17. Training the mind to do many things at once

Many people, when they begin the Fusion practice, say, "Oh! This is so difficult, there are so many things to do." But I say that it is simple. My mind is focused on the tan tien, and on the solar plexus, and on the Door of Life, and it is extended to the universe, all at the same time (fig. 2.18). It takes a diligent practice to gain confidence in the Fusion meditation. You can learn more about this practice in the book *Cosmic Fusion*.

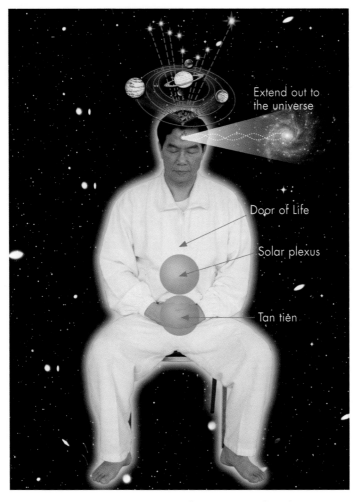

Fig. 2.18. Fusion: Focus on the tan tien, solar plexus,
Door of Life, and extend out to the universe.

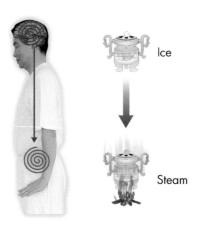

Fig. 2.19. When the mind is
empty, the ice will change
to steam.

Ice

Steam

Fig. 2.20. Warming the Stove

When the tan tien is warm, all the ice will begin to melt and the water will begin to change to steam (fig. 2.19). So the first thing you have to remember is to always focus on the tan tien, make the tan tien warm. We call this Warming the Stove (fig. 2.20). When you empty the mind, and thought arises, just smile down and relax. When you move your mind to other places, you still have to keep the tan tien warm. That is very important. When you begin to do this, you begin to see healing, and many things in the body begin to happen.

Wisdom Chi Kung Explanation

BRAIN-WAVE ACTIVITY

Scientists have recently discovered the same thing that the ancient Taoists discovered long ago. When human beings' left and right brain hemispheres are synchronized, they can double or triple their mind power, immediately.

We now have many different techniques both for measuring the different brain wave frequencies (see fig. 3.1 on page 30) and for synchronizing the brain waves in the left and right hemispheres. When I was being tested in Vienna for my brain-wave activity (which I will describe in detail in the next section), the scientists realized that when I smiled to the left and right kidneys and made the left and right kidney energies balance (the Door of Life)—one fire kidney, one water kidney, balancing in this way—the left and right kidney energy actually rises up and charges the left and right brain hemispheres. I can feel the connection when the energy charges into the left and right brain. When smiling to the sexual organs, the energy will charge the central part of the back of the brain.

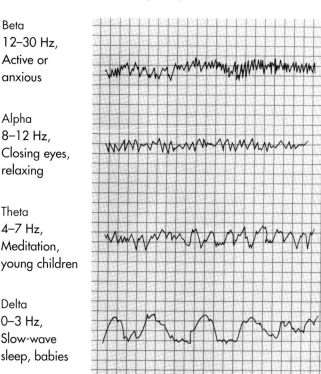

Beta
12–30 Hz,
Active or
anxious

Alpha
8–12 Hz,
Closing eyes,
relaxing

Theta
4–7 Hz,
Meditation,
young children

Delta
0–3 Hz,
Slow-wave
sleep, babies

1 sec

Fig. 3.1. Brain wave activity chart

MASTER CHIA CASE STUDY

In 1996, I was invited to go to the Institute for Biocybernetics and Feedback Research in Vienna for a study the doctors and scientists were doing on brain-wave activity measurements, using meditative frequencies. They were measuring brain-wave activity, brain energy, muscle tension, and blood pressure, and comparing the results with similar testing of professional athletes and others involved in sports. The researchers found that the athletes they studied cannot generate a lot of energy, and they hold a lot of tension in the muscles. They had great difficulty understanding the Taoist system of yin and yang and the healing properties of the practice, but they discovered that when

I am relaxing and smiling down to my abdomen, there is no muscle tension at all.

When there is a lot of muscle tension and the heart beats fast, the body cannot retain energy because the energy is always being used up just to perform daily activities, such as talking, sitting, or working. When there is very little muscle tension, the energy can keep on rising up. The circulation and blood pressure is low, and the pulse rate is also low. When you contract the anus, draw the energy up, and charge the brain, the energy level keeps on increasing. In this way, I have trained my body through these practices to generate energy and keep it rising (fig. 3.2).

When my body is very relaxed and I smile into my organs, the energy level in the body is about sixty units. When I smile to the sexual organ and raise the orgasmic arousal energy, it charges into

Fig. 3.2. Relax your muscles and raise energy with no tension.

the brain—and the energy level suddenly jumps to six thousand units. The researchers taking the measurements that showed this effect said, there is no way any person can have that level of energy in their brain; if anyone were to do this, the brain would "burn up." Their big question was, "How can Master Chia go from such a low level to such a high level so quickly?" I told them, "That is the healing energy in Taoist practices. That is the yin, in the yin and yang." The Tao practice is always yin relaxing and charging this yang energy up to the brain (fig. 3.3).

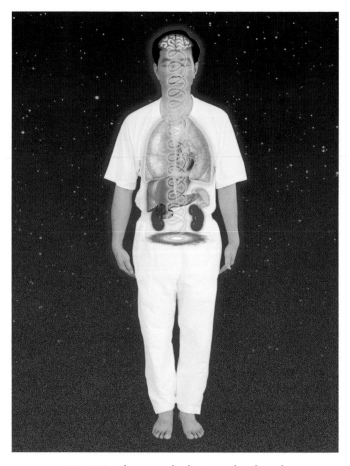

Fig. 3.3. Charging the brain with relaxed
energy is healing.

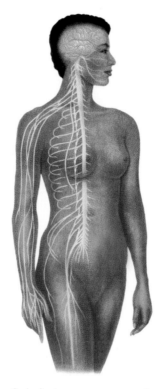

Fig. 3.4. A strong nervous system is
stress free.

In this research project, the doctors and scientists concluded that if you can develop your nervous system and then control it so that no stress in the world affects you and no one can stress you out, then your body can be full of energy and relaxed at the same time. I believe that no one else can actually stress another—it is how we respond that affects us.

When your nervous system is strong, no stress can get through to you (fig. 3.4). You can take a lot of stress, and it cannot penetrate your body, so you are stress free. For me, this all comes from practice of the Inner Smile, from the energy rising up into the brain, and from growing the energy within. When you draw the energy in, the rise in energy can happen very quickly.

DIFFERING POTENTIALS OF BRAIN ENERGY AND BRAIN-WAVE ACTIVITY

Researchers were also testing another group. This group comprised meditators who were working on learning how to send energy out of their bodies and receive energy back. When they received the energy back, the energy level in the brain actually rose; but when they stopped doing their practice they could not hold this energy level, and very quickly the level dropped to the original state. They were seeking some method that would allow them to hold the energy.

Some group members had heard me describing energy practices that matched exactly how they were trying to work with energy. So I went to their group and did a series of measurements along with them. We simply did the Inner Smile, smiling down to the abdomen, and very quickly they raised the charges in their energy measurements. The brain-wave activity was going lower and lower very quickly, nearly into a sleeping state, and at the same time the muscle tension was very low, the heart rate was low, and the skin resistance was very low.

At some point, I surged the energy up to the brain. The energy actually charged up into the brain so quickly that everyone looked at me with startled expressions, and someone asked, "What are you doing?" I said, "I'm smiling to my abdomen." As the researchers continued talking with me while they went on taking measurements, they discovered that I was responding to their questions while my brain-wave activity remained at the same low level. The recorded level indicated a resting state (fig. 3.5). By now, all were curious to know how I could answer their questions in this state of mind. In effect, according to the measurements, I was conversing with them while I was asleep.

It was only at this time that I began to understand. The whole practice of the Tao runs along the same thread, all having to do with training the second brain. It was at this point in time that I discovered the article on the second brain, or gut brain, quoted in chapter 2, and realized that my Tao masters had been training me to use the second brain in my abdomen the entire time (fig. 3.6).

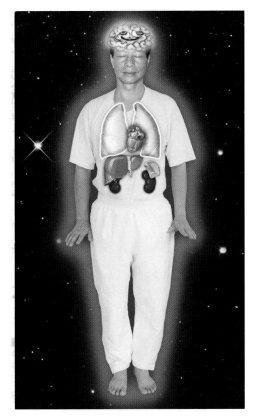

Fig. 3.5. Smiling the brain waves into a
resting state

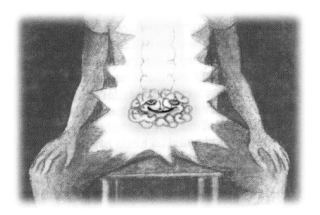

Fig. 3.6. Taoist masters discovered the second brain.

DIFFERING FUNCTIONS OF
THE TWO BRAINS

Western science has taken a long time to recognize the existence of this second brain. Recent studies, with results described in journal articles and other published materials, have attested to this complex brain in the abdomen, which not only controls the intricate process of digestion and many other bodily functions, but also interacts with the brain in the head (fig. 3.7). It sends messages in response to stimuli received from the head's brain, proving that this gut brain can process and respond to information (fig. 3.8). Research also indicates that the gut brain can record what it receives, storing that information permanently; and it can respond to emotional stimuli.

Originally, this research centered on the large and small intestines. But more recent research has included other organs, particularly the

 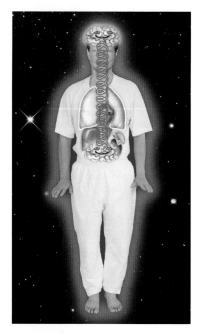

Fig. 3.7. The second brain controls the complex process of digestion and many other bodily functions.

Fig. 3.8. The second brain interacts with the brain in the head and sends messages in response to stimuli received from that brain.

heart. The heart can record and store the entire record of an event, and it has its own brain.

The Heart's Code, a book written by psychologist Paul Pearsall, describes how, when an individual undergoes a heart transplant operation and receives a new heart, he or she also receives with it the memories, experiences, and emotions from the previous individual whose heart it was. A particularly dramatic example described in the book involves a boy who was brutally murdered by an unknown assassin. His heart, however, was not injured and was transplanted to another boy in need of a new heart. Immediately after his recovery from the transplant operation, the eleven-year-old boy began to have recurring nightmares in which he experienced a brutal killing. He was able, while awake and remembering his dream, to describe the person who had killed him in the dream.

Eventually, his parents took him to the police, where a trained artist, based on the boy's description, reproduced the image of the individual in the dream. This led to the identification of the first boy's killer and, finally, to his capture and his confession of the murder. This example shows how the heart can record details of any and all experiences (fig. 3.9).

Fig. 3.9. The heart, like the second brain, has memory.

Wisdom Chi Kung practice can help anyone develop the capacity to use the processing and storing ability in their abdominal brain. You might ask, "Why is this so important?" The real reason lies in the differing ways that the two brains function. Often, we are using our head brain to do tasks for which the abdominal brain is much better suited. We also suffer from an inability to turn off our "monkey mind" when we are not using it, and this results in noise in the head and wasteful activity without any useful purpose. Monkey mind consumes enormous amounts of energy (fig. 3.10). As mentioned, the head brain is the big energy-spender in the body and can use up to 80 percent of total body energy. When this unneeded activity causes excess or negative emotions like worry, anger, hatred, fear, jealousy, sadness, or even joy, then its interaction with the second brain in the gut can cause serious disruption, leading to illness and disease.

This activity can go on, nonstop, for years! Just one single word or image can result in hours of brain activity; and one negative word or image can stimulate this activity for days, weeks, and even a life-

Fig. 3.10. The monkey mind consumes vital life-force energy.

time. In our "information age," there is continuous stimulation and input into this head brain of ours. This further increases the pressure on us to process information, leading to further reduction in our use of the gut brain, and eventually complete disassociation and disconnection between the two. Obviously, learning skills that will help us consciously interact with our innate system would be enormously beneficial for everyone.

Even when we utilize the thought processes that are among the real purposes of the head brain—for instance, planning, decision making, and the deduction of logical choices—we often limit our success by confusing the issues with other unrelated brain activity, like the processing of emotions (fig. 3.11). But this information is incomplete when we are not using the element of intuition or healing; thus, these seemingly logical processes have no significance in the support of the second brain. When the incessant first-brain activity blocks the more intricate signals from the second brain, on which these instinctive responses are based, we are robbed of the most valuable and powerful neurological biostructure we possess (fig. 3.12).

Fig. 3.11. Negative input depletes clarity.

Fig. 3.12. Too much first-brain activity blocks second-brain functioning.

The center of brain function really depends on the individual's type. Some very physical people use very little of their brainpower, but their physical bodies consume a lot of energy (fig. 3.13). People who are more focused on releasing energy through the body, rather than the mind, experience less stimulation to the brain and more of the relationship to the body. The problem here can be that the body is then tense and restricting the flow of neural connections throughout the body.

However, what we find more often is that people are using up huge amounts of their energy with the nonstop monkey-mind thinking. This leaves only a small percentage of the total energy for all the organs and the rest of the body to use.

The research on the gut brain has led many scientists and others to the conclusion that the actual "higher" functions of the head

Fig. 3.13. Athletes can transfer their brainpower into their bodies.

brain can in fact be done by the abdominal brain, with much less energy, and possibly with better, more reliable, and more harmonious results. Certain innate systems, including what we call intuition, hunch feelings, and such, are the true and appropriate functions of the gut brain (fig. 3.14). We are all familiar with the saying, "I have a gut feeling."

For activities involving these functions, the gut brain may be the only choice; it can in fact be called the emotional or feeling brain (fig. 3.15). In Taoist practice we are developing this gut feeling—this ability to feel or sense from the gut—into a conscious process. In order to accomplish this, the head brain must become quiet enough for the signals from the gut to connect with the brain, to be heard above the noise of the monkey mind. We must learn to quiet or idle the brain and let it rest. When this mind is still enough, we must

Fig. 3.14. Intuition arises from the gut ("gut feeling").

Fig. 3.15. The second brain is the "emotional brain."

Fig. 3.16. Learn to quiet the mind and allow the brain to function appropriately.

learn to allow the abdominal brain to function properly, and leave the head brain to do its intrinsically suited tasks with its particular capabilities (fig. 3.16).

The head brain often wants to take over all functioning. But we must properly develop the activities of the gut brain, such as simple awareness, consciousness, and interpersonal relations involving issues such as trust. Training the brain to trust the gut to do these tasks does involve some effort and technique.

BRAIN MEASUREMENT AND THE UNIVERSAL TAO

The Taoists began this kind of brain training centuries ago. Today, the Universal Tao system has proved itself, in the Western view, as a sufficient method to activate the internal modalities in the two brains, in order to gain the trust and communication we need.

Let us return briefly to Vienna, where the Institute for Biocybernetics and Feedback Research took on this project of meditative research. Dr. Gerhard Eggetsberger, the technical director of the institute, speaks of the results he found: "When Master Chia claims to move the chi in his body, the ultra slow potentials of brain-wave activity on my chi measurement device activate in waveforms that I have never seen before in any other system of meditation." My response is that when I move the chi in my body, the machine reflects what I know is happening inside of me. When I focus on the tan tien, I feel the tan tien filling with chi and the chi rising to the brain. Dr. Eggetsberger says, "The graph on my machine shows just what Master Chia says." After this experience, I am convinced that there is a direct correspondence between what this form of technology reflects and what I know is happening inside my body and mind.

Left and Right Brain Balancing

Throughout the testing, we discovered the right and left kidney activation and the sexual organ stimulation are directly affected with chi measurements (fig. 3.17). Many people who are right-handed, and heavily so, in their daily routine, go to test the energy in the brain and

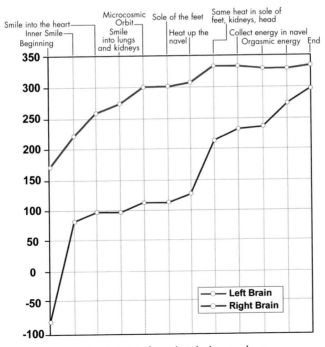

Fig. 3.17. Left and right brain chart

find that the left brain is very active while the right brain activity is very low. The difference can be as significant as half the measurable activity in the right brain as in the left.

Left-handed people are usually more creative, have active imaginations, and do a lot of dreaming and fantasizing, and in these people the right brain activity is very high and the left brain is very low. The two halves of the brain are never active to the same level.

In the Wisdom Chi Kung practices, we learn to develop the weaker side of the brain by charging the entire brain with chi and holding it in proper amounts. When just enough is charged to the brain, it can use this energy to balance itself, expand its capabilities, and in some cases, grow.

Expanding the Brain

Many studies in the West have proven that people who think hard, doing work that exercises their brain continuously, gradually over time develop more brain power. Unfortunately, what often happens in young adults is that the brain develops to a certain point and then the development stops. The Wisdom Chi Kung practice shows that you can develop the brain capacity, increase memory and thinking ability, and improve the level of abilities from young adulthood.

In Germany, some research has shown recently that people who are involved in work that requires much heavy thinking are in fact exercising the brain; this "workout" actually starts to expand the skull and push the cranium out. The same process can occur with the practices described in this book, because when you fill the brain with energy, the brain gets bigger. The work of many Taoist masters has shown this for thousands of years (fig. 3.18).

Normally, as people get older, the brain begins to shrink down as it consumes the energy available to it. The brain actually drinks this energy. With Wisdom Chi Kung based on the ancient Taoist practices, the older you get the bigger your brain will get. When the brain is filled with energy it will not shrink down.

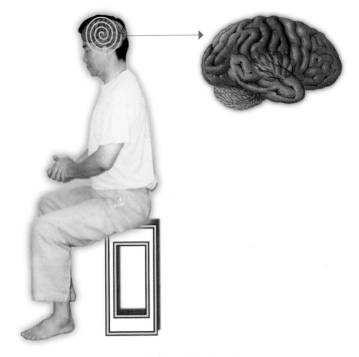

Fig. 3.18. Energy in the brain leads to brain expansion.

Jesus and Buddha

Now we are going to talk about the heart (fig. 3.19). We know that images play a very important role in our lives. That is why many organized religions build statues, beautiful temples, and churches. Much energy goes into these images, so that people can have a focus. When

Fig. 3.19. Forming the compassionate heart

people spend a lot of money building churches or temples, they have less energy and ability to build their own internal temples. The problem here is that the focus comes to rest on the outside rather than on the inside. The love for God is formed outside the self, and it focuses on these images.

I find it very interesting that Jesus, Buddha, and the other great spiritual masters never built a temple at all. Jesus and the Buddha spent many years just building their own internal temples. And Jesus said, "Your body is a temple" (fig. 3.20).

When I started teaching in America twenty-five years ago, many people thought the Universal Tao system was a very physically ori-

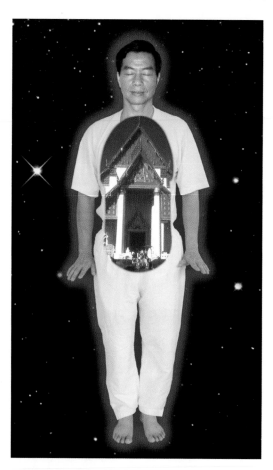

Fig. 3.20. Your body is your temple.

ented practice. Students were accustomed to practices that instructed them to always forget the body, focus on the universe only, smile to a statue, or praise God in Heaven. But as the ancient masters proclaimed, your body is the temple of God. Why focus on the buildings rather than on your body?

To begin the building of your temple, you can hold an image of the heart, picture the heart, smile to the heart. You are making a connection to the heart. Just making a connection you are starting to build up a temple within yourself. That is exactly what Jesus was saying—and holding an image of the organs is a very important step (fig. 3.21).

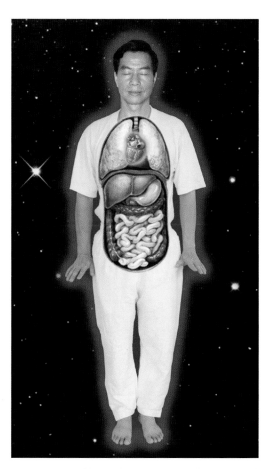

Fig. 3.21. Connect with your heart and build your temple within.

Organ Energy

The recent advancement in chi measurement technology has enabled researchers to analyze and assess the specific individual responses of organ energy. Before the most recent advances, during research, when I would smile down to my liver and the energy would rise up into the brain, the technology could only measure a slight rise in energy. I know that when I smile to the kidney, when I bring sunshine to the unfilled kidney, there is steam rising up, and the energy rises to the brain. At this point, a lot of energy charges into the brain but we cannot distinguish the specific region of the brain. Advancements in technology have their own limitations, so it is as important as ever to feel what is going on inside the body with no help at all. The level of energy in the brain represents the level of energy in the body.

FIVE ELEMENT ORGAN CORRESPONDENCES

	Wood	Fire	Earth	Metal	Water
Yin Organs	Liver	Heart	Spleen	Lungs	Kidneys
Yang Organs	Gallbladder	Small intestine	Stomach, pancreas	Large intestine	Bladder
Openings	Eyes	Tongue	Mouth, lips	Nose	Ears
Positive Emotions	Kindness	Love, joy	Fairness, openness	Righteousness, courage	Gentleness
Negative Emotions	Anger	Hate, impatience	Worry, anxiety	Sadness, depression	Fear, stress
Psychological Qualities	Control, decisiveness	Warmth, vitality, excitement	Ability to integrate, stabilize, center, and balance	Strength, substantiality	Ambition, willpower

 ## Taoist Meditation and Breathing to Begin Wisdom Chi Kung

Before beginning every practice, we must be able to see and expand our breath. Every time we sit down for meditation, this preparation is essential. Therefore, we begin by learning how to do this. In chapter 4 we will do the Spinal Cord Breathing in the sitting position.

1. Sit on the sitz bones, on the edge of the chair, spine erect, feet placed on the ground. In this position, the lumbar will be open and the energy can circulate (fig. 3.22). This way, you can rock on the base of the spine. If you sit and cannot rock, it means you are sitting on the tailbone, which is not a good position when you want to let the energy and the communication flow. If you sit on the tailbone, you sit on the tongue!

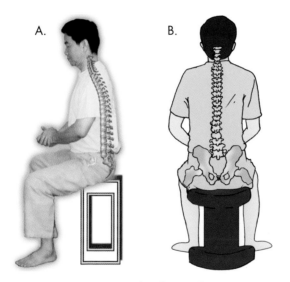

Fig. 3.22. (A) Sit on the chair with spine erect.
(B) Sit on the sitz bones and not the tailbone.

2. Inhale, exhale, inhale, exhale, in through the nose, out through the mouth, first 9 times, then 18 times, and lastly 36 times, resting briefly between repetitions. Imagine the breath pumping through the spine, elongating and expanding the vertebrae. Rock the kidneys, smile to the spine. This is a very peaceful practice. You do not have to do anything else—just sit, breathe, rock, and smile to the spine and the organs.

3. When you have finished the 36th repetition, rock the spine, one vertebra at a time, starting with the lumbar and working all the way up through the twenty-four stories to the cervical spine (fig. 3.23).

4. Rock the sacrum and the lumbar back and forth on the sitz bones to activate the sacral pump (fig. 3.24). We call this movement "Riding the Horse." Use only very small, internalized movements, so that it is more like a vibration rising up the spine from the base of the coccyx and the lower lumbar area, activating the sacral pump.

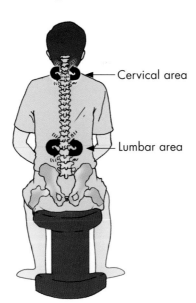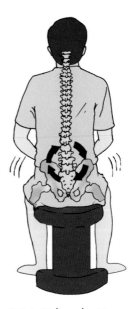

Fig. 3.23. Begin to rock the spine (lumbar to cervical), and smile into the organs.

Fig. 3.24. Riding the Horse: rock the lumbar to the sacral areas, activating the sacral pump.

This is a very useful practice; it creates good movement of the bones throughout the entire spine. When rocking this way, the vibration encourages the energy to move along the spine. Thus, this movement is especially good to use while practicing the Spinal Cord Breathing, which you will learn in chapter 4. Spinal cord breathing activates the three pumps: the sacrum, Door of Life, and cranial pump (fig. 3.25). When the lumbar spine and the Door of Life are open, the fluid can flow unrestricted and thereby feed sufficient nutrients back to the brain.

5. Activate the cranial pump with Crane Neck Rocking. (Chapter 4 describes the cranial pump in more detail.) Create a wavelike motion by loosely bending the middle and lower spine. While rocking, pay attention to the Door of Life and the L2 and L3 lumbar vertebrae. Feel the wave move from the lumbar spine up

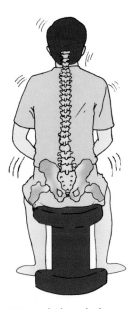

Fig. 3.25. Rock the whole spine and feel the energy vibration activate the three pumps.

to the neck. Start by arching L2 and L3 to the front as you stretch the neck to the back. Then stretch the neck like a crane. Reach the chin forward, curve it in, and touch it to the throat. At the same time, push back the lumbar area, creating a wavelike movement. Repeat this motion 18 to 36 times.

6. Press the tongue onto the roof of the mouth to activate the saliva (fig. 3.26). In the saliva, we find an important sign that the energy is moving. When the energy charges up to the brain and the brain starts to activate, it secretes a sweet fragrant substance that is very nourishing and healing for all the rest of the body. When the saliva comes out in a big rush—very sweet and fragrant—we no longer call it saliva, we call it nectar.

7. As the saliva moves, feel warmth coming back to the navel and the Door of Life. Move your hand to touch the navel. Remember to keep the tan tien warm and keep the Door of Life warm (fig. 3.27). Feel the connection at the tan tien, with the brain secreting

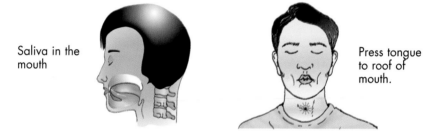

Saliva in the mouth

Press tongue to roof of mouth.

Fig. 3.26. Smile inside and activate the saliva nectar.

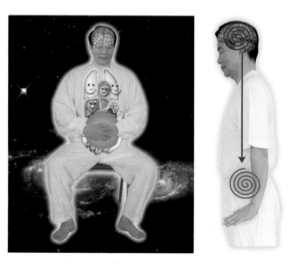

Fig. 3.27. Smile down, fill the tan tien with chi, empty the mind, relax and let go.

the sweet nectar. Feel the pumps activated and the organs smiling. Your eyes are like the sun, shining on the water (fig. 3.28).

8. Move your hand to your heart, activate the heart fire, and make your heart soft (fig. 3.29). Feel the love, feel joy, remember to keep the tan tien warm. The heart will charge energy right into

Fig. 3.28. The eyes are like the sun shining on the water.

Fig. 3.29. Soften the heart and keep smiling.

the center of the brain; this love and joy from the heart fills the brain and transforms negative energy. With the sun shining on the water, the water changes to steam. Remember to keep the tan tien warm.

Now we can integrate this sitting preparation into the beginning of the Wisdom Chi Kung practice, expanding and furthering the practice throughout the next chapter.

Wisdom Chi Kung Practice

In this chapter we present the bulk of the Wisdom Chi Kung practice. The first section describes three introductory breathing and energy activation exercises: Spinal Cord Breathing, Laughing to Activate the Tan Tien, and the Three Fires practice. The next section explains and illustrates the heart of the Wisdom Chi Kung practice. A final section combines and integrates the techniques.

PRELIMINARY PRACTICES

Spinal Cord Breathing

We do the first preliminary practice standing up. Spinal Cord Breathing is a method for activating the "three pumps" (see figs. 4.1 and 4.2 on page 56). The first of these pumps is the sacrum or sacral pump.

The sacrum must pump the fluid to cause it to flow up the spinal cord and to the brain. Activating this pump begins the perineal and sacral flow of energy and sustains this flow throughout the body, regulating the distribution of energy to all the different points along the meridians.

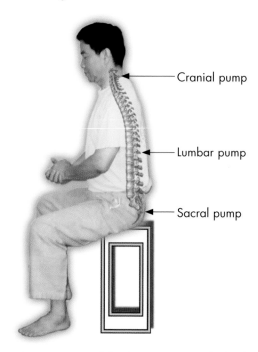

Fig. 4.1. Location of the three pumps in the body

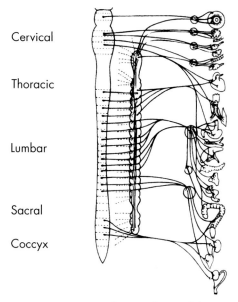

Fig. 4.2. The vertebrae of the spine

Because the human being stands erect, it takes a powerful pump, working against the force of gravity, to push the fluid all the way up to the brain. So the sitting position, especially when sitting on the sacrum, makes this very difficult. When you are sitting all the time, you are sitting on the sacrum—on your pump—and the fluid does not flow.

When the body ages, the flow of energy and fluid can decrease and may no longer provide enough nourishment to the brain and other parts of the body, and much capacity can be lost. That's why many older people begin to shrink: their bones actually start to shrivel and condense. There is little fluid for elasticity of the muscles and bones, creating a loss of mass of these parts. The brain "dries out," and often this is the reason for decreased mental capacity.

Learning to separate the sacral movement from the hip movement is important because they are very different movements. We really only see this movement in the pop stars in our society, who are making millions of dollars off of it. When people see the rock singers moving the sacrum like this, they feel sexually aroused; they feel so excited and free in the body that they begin to circulate this sexual energy.

The sacrum bone is also called the secret bone or sacred bone. Centuries ago, it was forbidden for "ordinary" people to see this movement of the sacrum. Priests taught the young virgin girls to dance for God, calling it a sacred dance, which, not surprisingly, only the priests themselves could watch.

In these "ceremonies," modern and ancient, when the sound of a drum is added, the heart activates and the sexual energy rises up; but often it jams in the brain. When the energy builds up but does not move, people go crazy or become obsessed, because this energy is constantly creating pressure on the brain. Also, much sexual frustration accumulates with this jamming because of the fantasy and dreaming created in the brain while the energy is not being expelled through the body.

So you need to practice rocking the sacrum back and forth from a standing position—first tucking the tailbone under, then letting it rock back. When you move in this way, you activate the sacral pump, which then begins to pump the fluid up the spinal cord.

The next pump is at the Door of Life, above the sacrum, at the lumbar section of the spine. When you start to rock both the sacrum and the Door of Life center at the same time, the fluid really begins to circulate. When the fluid circulates to these areas, your posture becomes more erect, your stance improves, and your height increases. By rocking and walking, these pumps become active, and the oxygen from your intake of breath will induce appropriate movement of the blood in this area.

Moving up, the next pump is what we call the cranial pump. The opening part of the Spinal Cord Breathing movement is to lower the chin down and pull it back while you move the sacrum as well. This opens up the neck, cranial sutures, muscles, and parathyroid and thyroid glands, and also opens up the lungs for increased oxygen. Practice rocking the neck back and forth 36 times, inhaling and exhaling with each movement. Because the neck and cranium are so intrinsically connected, by activating one, you automatically activate the other.

The cranial-sacral movement has been studied for a long time now, and there are some specific forms of bodywork and healing methods that focus only on this flow between the two pumps. The flow is actually a fluid encased in a sac called the dura mater. This fluid lubricates the cranium, the vertebrae of the entire spine, and areas around the sacrum and pelvis.

The cranial-sacral connection is like having pulleys at the head and the sacrum, with a rope connecting the two. When you pull on one end of the rope, the other is activated, but pulled in the opposite direction. By feeling the pulls of the Spinal Cord Breathing movement, you can increase the healthy flow of the craniosacral fluid and improve the alignment of the corresponding bones and muscles.

Many times as children, we fall on the tailbone, and the impact creates a dislocation between the tailbone and the sacrum. This then affects the way the sacrum and cranium connect with each other, often inhibiting the connection, and it takes much awareness and attention to appropriately make the connection again.

When you have made the spinal cord connection and all three pumps are activated, there is a natural flow of the energy through these pumps to stimulate chi and enliven the body.

Study the diagram carefully as you learn this exercise, and make sure you understand the exact movement (fig. 4.3). Look into a mirror to see that you are doing the movement correctly.

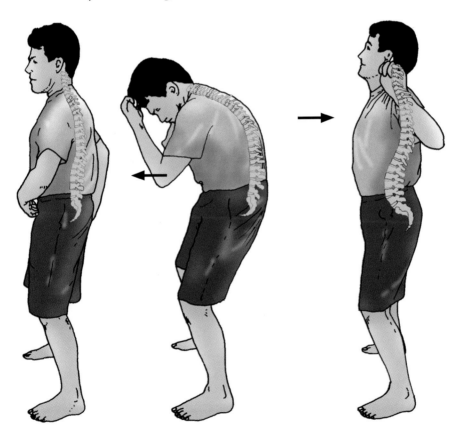

Fig. 4.3. Rock the sacrum, Door of Life, and cranium
back and forth.

Standing Spinal Cord Breathing to Activate the Three Pumps

1. Stand comfortably, with feet about hip width apart, knees slightly bent, arms bent at the elbows and extended to the sides of the body. Inhale and expand the chest (fig. 4.4).

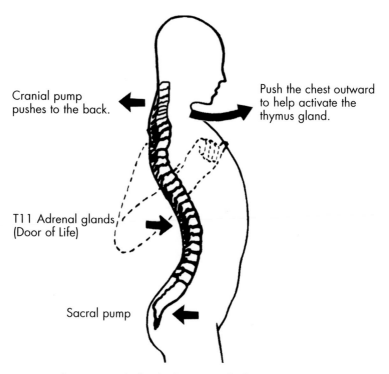

Cranial pump pushes to the back.

Push the chest outward to help activate the thymus gland.

T11 Adrenal glands (Door of Life)

Sacral pump

Fig. 4.4. The sacrum tilts back, the Door of Life pushes to the front, the sternum also pushes to the front, and the cranial pump pushes to the back.

2. Exhale, lower the chin down and pull it in, tuck the tailbone under you, and round the back, bringing the elbows toward one another in the front of the chest (fig. 4.5).
3. Smile, inhale again, expand the chest, tuck the chin in toward the throat, push the chin back and raise the crown, and bring the arms out toward the sides.

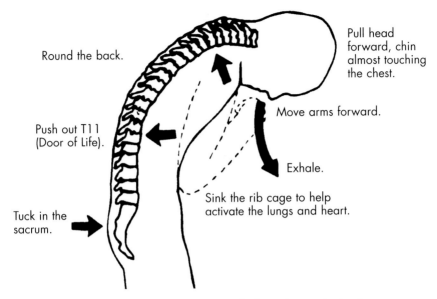

Round the back.

Pull head forward, chin almost touching the chest.

Push out T11 (Door of Life).

Move arms forward.

Exhale.

Tuck in the sacrum.

Sink the rib cage to help activate the lungs and heart.

Fig. 4.5. The sacrum tucks, the Door of Life pushes to the back, the sternum tucks in and the chin tucks as the cranial sutures open.

4. Repeat this movement 36 times. This movement activates the cranial and sacral pumps, and loosens all the joints along the length of the spine.

Breath and Laughter

I have sat with many different masters over the long course of my study, and every one has given me at least one breathing technique. The Taoist texts naturally address the subject of the breath; but in addition, the Taoist texts always talk about a "drum" beating in the tan tien, like a vibration there. After many years of reading the Taoist texts and practicing all the different breathing techniques, I came to realize something. I realized that we have a natural, very effective, and powerful breathing technique, one that arises from the way we laugh. When our laughter is real, deep, and honest, that is the abdominal laugh.

When you learn this deep laughter, it activates the diaphragm. Taoism refers to this as the second heart. Especially during laughter, the active movement of the diaphragm causes a pumping effect, which gives the diaphragm the same kind of pumping action as the heart.

When people are sitting, and sitting for long periods of time, thinking and thinking, nearly two-thirds of the blood is stagnant in the organs. It does not move at all. This is one of the major causes of sickness. When you learn how to laugh, and the vibration in the tan tien is very strong, just like a heartbeat, this pumping helps to move the blood and the chi. With this help, the heart can pump much more easily. So, if you can activate the vibration in the tan tien, Taoism says it is like a second heart (fig. 4.6). And many good things are associated with this second heart.

Fig. 4.6. Activate the second heart by abdominal laughing.

Laughing to Activate the Tan Tien

We are going to learn and practice this laughing in three different ways.

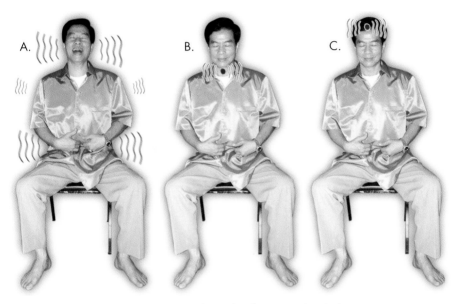

Fig. 4.7. (A) Laugh out loud. (B) Laugh a little.
(C) Laugh with the cranium.

1. Laugh out loud and feel the vibrations created by your laughter (fig. 4.7a).
2. Laugh as though you are in church and suddenly something strikes you as very funny, but you cannot laugh loudly. Feel the higher vibration in the throat (fig. 4.7b).
3. Laugh with the cranium, in silence. It's as though something right in front of you is so funny, so wonderfully amusing, that you have the feeling of laughter very big inside of you (fig. 4.7c). Feel it like a drum beating and vibrating deep inside.

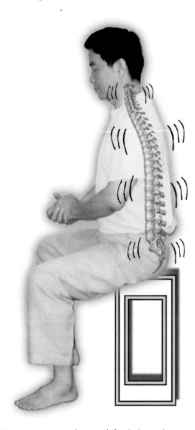

Fig. 4.8. Laugh, and feel the vibration
of love filling your spine.

As you learn to laugh deep inside, feel that the laughter is vibrating tremendously inside you. When you do this, the blood, the chi, the energy are all moving. So the stagnant chi is gone, and the most important pump, the heart, can work with less effort (fig. 4.8).

Introduction to the Three Fires

With the natural connection of the laughter activating the second heart and establishing the vibration in the tan tien, we start smiling down, to introduce the activation of the three fires.

Activation of the Three Fires

To activate the three fires you must inhale the smiling energy and exhale it down to the tan tien.

1. Feel the smiling energy in front of you.
2. Lift up the corners of the mouth, and empty your mind.
3. Keep on smiling, and empty your mind down to the tan tien.
4. Fix on a point in the abdominal area, and just keep smiling down. Once you get to a certain level, the tan tien starts to get warm. When your smile has warmed the tan tien, the first fire has started—the fire burning under the sea (fig. 4.9).

Fig. 4.9. First fire activated: the tan tien fire

5. Touch the navel and focus on this area—the Door of Life—and feel the Door of Life warm. Now there is a fire burning here. This is the kidney fire activating. The kidney fire is so essential because it is the original force (fig. 4.10). We are born with this force and we use it continuously throughout our lifetime. The Taoists believe that when this force is drained out, your life force is finished.

The kidney fire is actually involved with the sexual energy. This fire is burning every day, and when it goes out, you die.

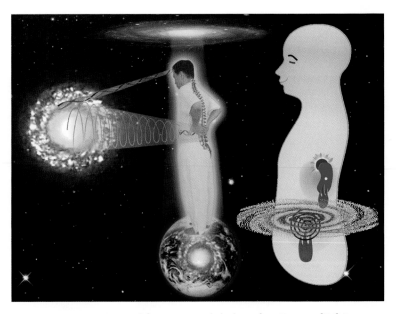

Fig. 4.10. Second fire activated: kidney fire (Door of Life)

6. Now move your hands to your heart and keep smiling down. Feel the heart fire activate, the loving energy, the compassion energy, and when you feel the heart fire burning, make it soft—very, very soft (fig. 4.11).

7. Keep emptying the mind down, down, to activate the energy (fig. 4.12). You will begin to feel it when something actually charges up to the brain. In the beginning, you might feel something like

Fig. 4.11. Third fire activated: heart fire

Fig. 4.12.
Activation of the
three fires: tan tien,
kidney, and heart

Fig. 4.13. Brain activation as a result of
the fire activation

a numbness in the brain. Then the energy begins to rebuild and repair, and you start to develop new brain power (fig. 4.13).

Now that you are aware of your breath and the essential focuses of the practice, we can move on to the heart of the Wisdom Chi Kung.

THE HEART OF THE WISDOM CHI KUNG PRACTICE

In all the meditative practices in the world, the first step is to get the energy flowing. Whether you are chanting, praying, singing, focusing on a mantra or an icon, or whatever, there will always be instructions like this. All these practices have various starting patterns to focus and move the energy. But the goal is always energy.

In the Universal Tao, we do not have all these other patterns in

Fig. 4.14. Taoist practices charge the entire being with energy.

front; we go directly into the main practices and techniques to induce the spiritual flow (fig. 4.14). In order to understand how to get this movement, we must have an explanation of the heart of the practice, so here, we are dedicated to doing just this.

The Wisdom Chi Kung Practice

Continue to bring your focus and awareness to the tan tien and the activated fires in the body. This will allow you to increase your energy more and more. The continued focus is the key to this practice. If it helps you to focus, touch each energy center with your hand.

When you empty your mind into your organs, you will have extra energy with which to repair and heal the body. When the mind is empty, energy that has been transformed in the organs can charge back up to the brain. You can use the Inner Smile to help charge this energy back up to the brain. This transformed energy will now work to repair the brain, increase the memory, and expand mental capacity.

Ultimately, you can combine chi and intention with the universal energy. It will be returned to you multiplied many times, to fill you with enhanced life force.

Activate the Three Fires

1. Smile down and empty the mind to the lower tan tien, the abdominal brain (fig. 4.15).
2. Touch the tan tien; fill the tan tien with chi. Wisdom arises from the awareness and sense of appropriateness created when the head brain and the abdominal brain connect (fig. 4.16).
3. Activate the tan tien fire—the Fire under the Sea—to transform the chi (fig. 4.17).
4. Touch the navel area. Smile down to the Door of Life and activate the kidney fire there (fig. 4.18). This is the original force, the True Fire. Always retain awareness at the tan tien.

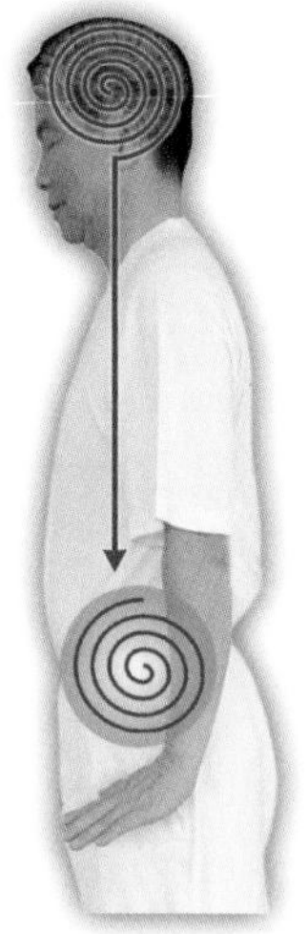

Fig. 4.15. Smile down to the tan tien.

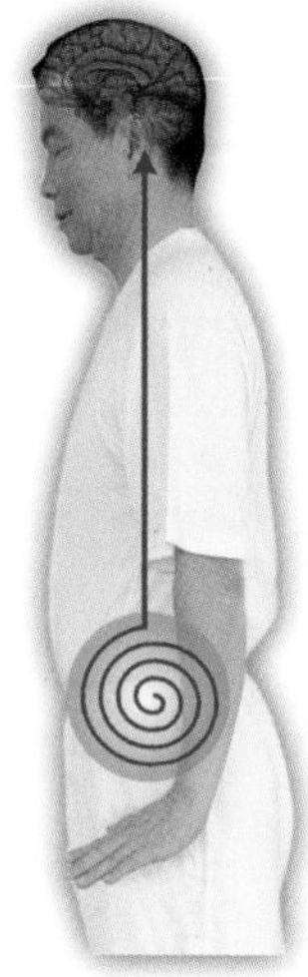

Fig. 4.16. Fill the tan tien with chi.

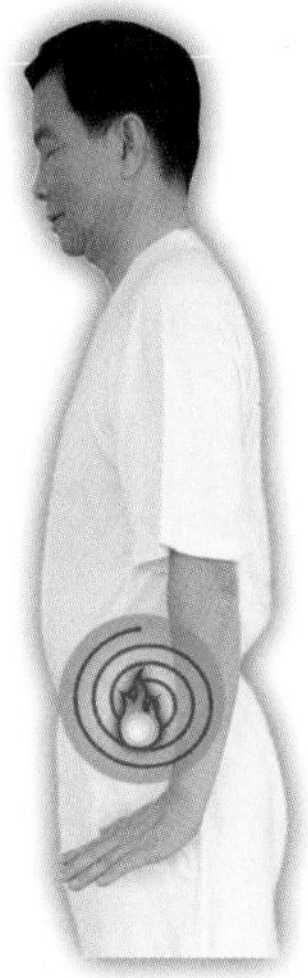

Fig. 4.17. Activate the tan tien fire (the Fire under the Sea).

Fig. 4.18. Activate the kidney fire (the original force,
the True Fire).

5. Smile down to the heart and keep smiling until you feel the heart
   fire activate (fig. 4.19). This is the Imperial Fire. Keep the heart
   very soft, and feel love, joy, and happiness.

Fig. 4.19. Activate
the heart fire (the
Imperial Fire).

❂ Smile Down to the Organs to Transform Chi

1. Smile to the kidneys. Continue to empty the mind to the tan tien and the kidneys (fig. 4.20).
2. Keep 95 percent of the attention at the tan tien, and 5 percent smiling to the kidneys. When the kidneys are filled, transformed chi will rise up and fill the back part of the brain (fig. 4.21). The left and right sides of the back of the brain both fill with kidney chi (fig. 4.22).

Fig. 4.20.
Smile to the
kidneys.

Fig. 4.21.
Transformed
chi rises from
the kidneys
to fill the
back of the
brain.

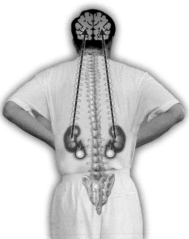

Fig. 4.22.
Kidney chi fills
both sides of
the back of the
brain.

3. Smile, relax, empty the mind down to the bladder and sexual organs, and allow these organs to store and transform the chi (fig. 4.23).

    The transformed chi will rise up and fill the center part of the brain with chi (fig. 4.24).

4. Smile, relax, and empty the mind down to the liver and gallbladder. Let them transform the chi (fig. 4.25).

    Chi that has been transformed in the liver will rise up and fill the center of the right brain (fig. 4.26).

Fig. 4.23. Smile down to the bladder and sexual organs. These organs can store and transform chi.

Fig. 4.24. Transformed chi rises from the bladder and sexual organs to the center of the brain.

Fig. 4.25. Smile down to the liver and gallbladder.

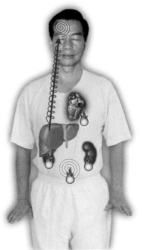

Fig. 4.26. Transformed chi rises from the liver to the center of the right brain.

5. Smile, relax, empty the mind into the heart and small intestine (fig. 4.27). The heart and small intestine can store and transform chi.

   Chi transformed in the heart and small intestine will charge up and fill the front part of the center of the brain (fig. 4.28).

6. Smile, relax, empty the mind down to the stomach, spleen, and pancreas (fig. 4.29). Keep 95 percent of the attention on the tan tien.

   Chi transformed in the stomach, spleen, and pancreas will charge the left brain with energy (fig. 4.30).

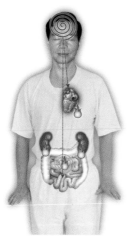

Fig. 4.27. Smile down to the small intestine.

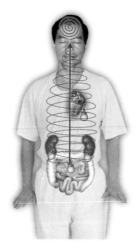

Fig. 4.28. Transformed chi rises from the heart and small intestine to fill the front part of the center of the brain.

Fig. 4.29. Smile down to the stomach, spleen, and pancreas.

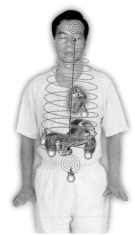

Fig. 4.30. Transformed chi rises from the stomach, spleen, and pancreas to fill the left brain with energy.

7. Relax, smile, empty the mind down to the lungs and large intestine (fig. 4.31).

    Chi transformed in the lungs and large intestine will rise up and fill the front part of the left and right brain (fig. 4.32).

8. Continue to empty the mind down to the tan tien and all the organs. Remember to keep 95 percent of the focus on the tan tien (fig. 4.33).

    When the mind is empty, the transformed chi from the tan tien and the organs can charge up to fill the brain with energy (fig. 4.34).

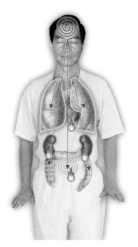

Fig. 4.31. Smile down to the lungs and large intestine.

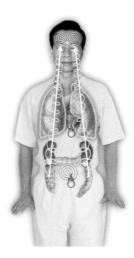

Fig. 4.32. Transformed chi rises from the lungs and large intestine to fill the front part of the left and right brain.

Fig. 4.33. Continue to empty the mind down to the tan tien and organs.

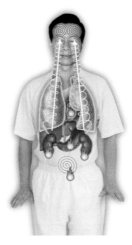

Fig. 4.34. When the mind is empty, then it can be filled with transformed chi.

❁ Combine Your Chi with the Universal Energy

1. Now that your brain is filled with the transformed chi, become aware of a star or light above you. Always maintain your awareness of the tan tien (fig. 4.35).
2. Become aware of the universe, with the stars and the galaxies in it (fig. 4.36). Smile and empty the mind to the universe. Relax and let go, and be completely empty.

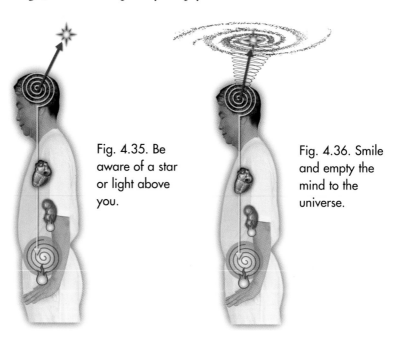

Fig. 4.35. Be aware of a star or light above you.

Fig. 4.36. Smile and empty the mind to the universe.

3. As you maintain awareness of the universe, touch it with your mind; touch the stars and galaxies in it (fig. 4.37). Continue to be aware of the tan tien so you do not lose yourself.
4. Open yourself to contain the universe. Combine the universal energy with the transformed chi at the tan tien (fig. 4.38). This is the secret of all the great masters.
5. Combine your chi and good intention with the high universal energy and let this multiply while retaining a majority of your awareness at the tan tien (fig. 4.39).

Fig. 4.37. Touch the universe with your mind.

Fig. 4.38. Open yourself to the universe. Combine the universal energy with the transformed chi at the tan tien.

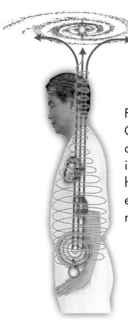

Fig. 4.39. Combine your chi and good intention with the high universal energy, and let it multiply.

6. Remain focused and steady, and allow the universal energy, now blended with your own chi, to pour into you. The energy will return to you multiplied many times, to fill the brain and the whole body (fig. 4.40).

7. Hold the enhanced chi in the brain for as long as it remains comfortable (fig. 4.41). As your practice deepens, you will be able to hold it longer.

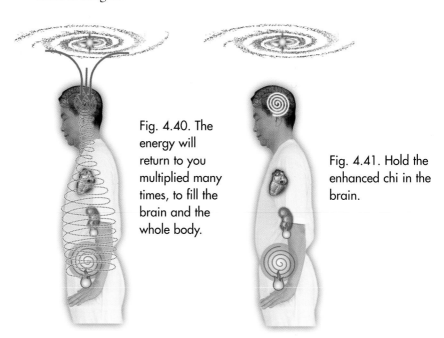

Fig. 4.40. The energy will return to you multiplied many times, to fill the brain and the whole body.

Fig. 4.41. Hold the enhanced chi in the brain.

8. Empty the mind down to the tan tien once again (fig. 4.42). Feel the enhanced energy fill the tan tien with a higher frequency of chi. This chi will be further refined and enhanced and available to fill the brain again.

9. Once the brain has been filled again, empty the mind once more to the universe. When it is empty, the mind will be filled with a higher force, which will open the capacity for increased understanding and wisdom (fig. 4.43).

Fig. 4.42. Empty the mind down to the tan tien once again. Then allow the refined, high-frequency chi to fill the brain again.

Fig. 4.43. Empty the mind once more to the universe. Accept the flow of a higher force, increasing your understanding and wisdom.

Integration

Allow yourself a moment to feel the practice. Notice any differences in your body, mind, heart; compare how you felt when you began the practice with how you feel now. The difference may be clear, or it may be subtle to begin with. In any case, just notice and bring your attention to what has altered. As you consistently expand the practice, the subtleties will increase, and your awareness of the chi that is flowing through your body will enhance dramatically.

As you "check in" with yourself at this moment, reflect on any other thought processes that occurred during your practice. Notice the activity of the monkey mind, and quietly thank and tell that part of your consciousness that it is no longer needed during this time of meditation. Be gentle with yourself. Allow yourself ample time to familiarize and grasp the Wisdom Chi Kung practice. Remember that every mighty oak tree starts as a seed.

INTEGRATING WISDOM CHI KUNG:
ENDING THE PRACTICE

Now that you have been introduced to the Wisdom Chi Kung system, it is important to make a connection with the different aspects of the practices—to combine and integrate—for a more complete understanding.

In the preliminary practices, we felt the breath increase by internally activating the three pumps and the three fires, and by feeling the sensations and effects of laughter in the body. Let us come full circle by returning to the healing laughter before we smile down to integrate the practices.

 ## Integrating the Practices

Everyone knows laughing lightens the spirit. But do we always have to have a reason to laugh? The answer is no. You can laugh without a reason; and it is actually very important to do so.

Once you start laughing, hearing yourself laugh will make you laugh even more. Especially when you're by yourself! Sometimes I think how hilarious it is that I am alone and laughing at nothing. But I am actually laughing at myself laughing at nothing, and that's quite funny. Thus I end up laughing even harder!

So, before you begin the last meditation, try laughing with no reason. If you are feeling too serious or too emotional, try recording the sound of laughter. Loud laughing on tape is actually quite catching.

Put your hands on the navel, and once again experience the sensations of laughter in your entire being (fig. 4.44). Laugh loud, then softer, and finally give yourself a little giggle as if you just remembered one of the most embarrassing times of your life.

1. Put your hands down over the navel. Smile, and keep a slight smile on your face. Begin to feel the very subtle smiling energy all around you.

Fig. 4.44. Feel the laughing, giggling, smiling energy deep inside.

2. Inhale, exhale, and feel the breath sinking down. Keep smiling, relaxing, breathing, sinking the breath down to the tan tien. Keep reminding yourself: empty the mind down, fill the tan tien with chi. If the mind is wandering around, fix the mind on the lower tan tien, breathing the mind down, continuing to smile (fig. 4.45).

Fig. 4.45. Bring the wandering mind back with the breath and into the tan tien.

3. With one hand touching the navel, invite your awareness to feel the three fires activated: the tan tien, the Door of Life, and the Imperial Fire. Keep smiling down to the tan tien, the eyes like the sun shining on the water.

4. Move the hands down to cover the pelvic area, and smile down to the sexual organs. Picture the sexual organs. Inhale, exhale, relax, empty the mind down to the lower abdomen. Feel the sun shining on the water (fig. 4.46).

Fig. 4.46. Sun shining on the water, onto the three fires
and the sexual organs

5. Now move the hands to the navel, and just start spiraling the energy. Do not worry about the direction. Feel the energy being stored in the navel area. When the energy in the navel grows warm, you will feel the energy begin to charge up to the brain (fig. 4.47).

6. Press the tongue to the roof of the mouth. As the energy charges up to the brain, the next thing you are going to get is a lot of saliva, very sweet saliva, or nectar, coming down. Swallow this nectar down to the tan tien. This is a special form of nourishment from the brain (fig. 4.48).

Fig. 4.47. Feel the relaxed, charged energy fill
the brain with chi.

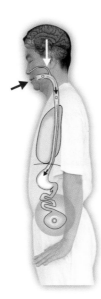

Fig. 4.48. Swallow the
sweet saliva, the nectar
from the brain, down to
the tan tien.

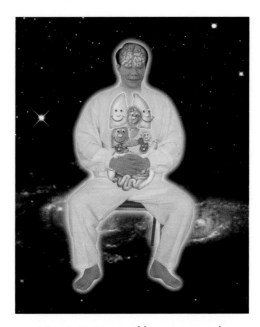

Fig. 4.49. Rest and be rejuvenated.

7. Rest, and feel the navel and lower tan tien increase in warmth. Feel the nourishment of the smile, the laughter, the relaxing breath, and the refined chi vibrating and rejuvenating your entire being (fig. 4.49).

Ending the Meditations

This very basic practice is the most important thing you can do in your life. Even when you learn the Universal Tao system to the highest level, this is the essential foundation. Every time you practice, you must do the same thing: Empty the mind, stop the brain, fill the tan tien with chi. Simple and effective, this practice is the most crucial.

Ending the meditations is perhaps the most important time of the meditations. This is the time when the body has to completely relax and assimilate everything that has occurred before and during the practice. This is the time when the body, mind, and spirit begin to integrate, fuse together, and unify the external with the internal.

This is the goal of the practice. This is why we do the practice: to be finished with it. When we are finished, we live our life, and the practice becomes a part of who we are, what we live for, what we learn and teach, how we talk and breathe. How we relate with others and how we relate with ourselves.

Take time at this very moment, sitting or standing, to feel yourself. Notice any changes, notice anything that has not changed. Just notice, and be gentle with yourself at this crucial stage of integration. When we are at this stage, our inner being begins to strengthen, and the spirit becomes stronger with awareness.

Awareness of our being allows our consciousness to expand. We become wiser. This is Wisdom Chi Kung. Empty the mind, raising the chi. The more we can do this, the more our wisdom increases to higher capacities. Generate energy, and at the same time be empty. This is Wisdom Chi Kung.

Feeding the First
and Second Brains
to Increase Wisdom

The human brain has the same number of cells from birth until death. Each brain cell has synapses that connect to many other similar cells (fig. 5.1). The brain is also filled with proteins, which, under normal conditions, the brain cannot fully utilize. If we raise the level of energy in the brain, and maintain the brain in this enhanced state for a period of time, at a certain point the brain cells can grow new synapses and increase the capacity of each cell.

Each day we use up much of the brain's available energy. As mentioned, when we are thinking or worrying too much, the brain can use up to about 80 percent of the entire body's energy, which leaves only 20 percent for the rest of the system (fig. 5.2). If we can stop the brain for a short moment, we can learn to increase mental capacity, focus, and clarity.

It is also essential that we rest and eat the right foods, so that we regain lost brainpower and maintain the brainpower that we still have. Our brainpower tends to diminish as we grow older, and thus it becomes ever more imperative to nourish the entire system to preserve and enhance what is left.

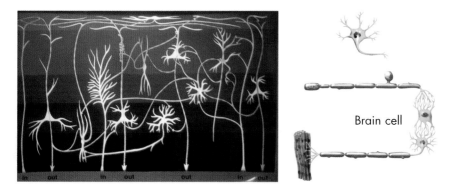

Brain cell

Fig. 5.1. Each brain cell has synapses that connect to many similar cells.

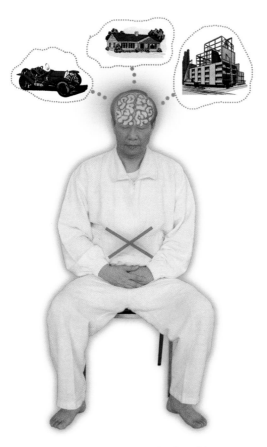

Fig. 5.2. Overusing the head brain
wastes too much of the body's life force.

NOURISHMENT FOR THE BRAIN

Each of the Universal Tao basic practices has the effect of raising your total energy level and recharging the brain with energy. To develop your capacity, you need to practice three times a day, holding chi in the brain and the spine. Start by activating the fire in the tan tien, opening the Microcosmic Orbit and generating wisdom. As you learn more, the sexual practice is the most powerful, including the Testicle and Ovarian Breathing practices and the Power Lock. (More on this subject can be found in *Taoist Cosmic Healing*.)

When you practice every day, the brain is adequately nourished and enough energy is being generated. The brain can then charge the entire system, the organs can store energy, and the sexual organs can produce a consistent flow of sexual energy (fig. 5.3).

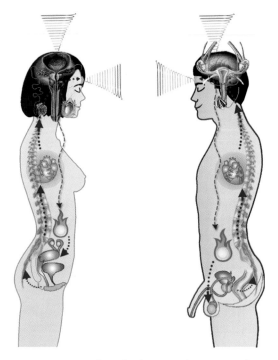

Fig. 5.3. Feeding the brain with energized
chi nourishes the body.

Brain Food

For the brain to function properly it must be provided with the proper nourishment. There are many ways to classify food. In the West, it is classified according to its chemical components.

1. **Amino acids** are the basic building blocks of the cells. Two of the amino acids in particular affect the functions of the brain:
   - **Tyrosine** comes primarily from the protein in meat, fish, poultry, eggs, and beans, and is used to manufacture the neurotransmitters responsible for alertness, mental control, quick thinking, fast reaction time, and long-term memory.
   - **Tryptophan** is found primarily in the protein of poultry, peanuts, and milk, but it needs carbohydrates to make it available to the brain. Tryptophan is responsible for the manufacturing of serotonin, a neurotransmitter that slows reaction time, causes sleepiness, impairs concentration, and reduces the need to be in control.
2. **Vitamins** are essential for the functioning of the brain. The carbohydrates and tryptophan, for example, will not produce serotonin in your brain unless they are combined with vitamin B$_6$. The other B vitamins also play an important part in brain functioning and in the ability of the brain to use the nourishment it receives. You can get these B vitamins by eating fish, poultry, grains, dark leafy greens, and eggs.
   - **Vitamin C** is another vitamin that experiments have shown increases the ability of the brain to use protein to make the neurotransmitters responsible for thinking and remembering. Vitamin C is essential in keeping the immune system clean, therefore keeping the body alert and healthy. For vitamin C, eat plenty of fruits (especially citrus) and vegetables.
3. **Essential fatty acids, Omega-3, -6, and -9,** provide the EPA and DHA that research has found to be essential nourishment

for the brain cells, the eyes, the heart, the liver, and semen. The polyunsaturated fats in combination also contribute to the ability of the brain to function well. DHA also supports the immune system function. The DHA in seafood helps the growth of the tips of the neurons (dendrites), and this creates new connections in the brain and helps transmit information between brain cells. This improves memory and learning ability. You can get the essential fatty acids by eating fish and shellfish, flaxseeds, sesame and other seeds, and sea vegetables.

These are a few of the chemical substances in our foods that provide optimum brain health and performance. Make sure to eat a balanced diet full of vitamins from fruits and vegetables, carbohydrates from grains and potatoes, and protein from fish, poultry, eggs, milk, grains, nuts, and seeds (fig. 5.4).

Fig. 5.4. Feeding the body with correct nutrition is essential for high performance of the first and second brains, and for that glowing energy.

A Balanced Diet

In the East, one way of classifying food is according to its energetic nature. A balanced diet is one that provides each organ with its own kind of energy. Each organ's energy also feeds primary energy to certain systems in the body. To nourish the body's various systems, you have to plan your meals accordingly. Thus, a balanced diet has equal parts of the following five tastes and colors:

The liver and gallbladder desire food that is green and sour tasting. This food feeds the nerves.

The heart and small intestine relish bitter tastes and food that is red. This food feeds the heart and its vessels.

The spleen, pancreas, and stomach desire food that is sweet. This food feeds the muscles. This does not mean adding sugar or sweeteners, but refers to food that is naturally sweet.

The lungs and large intestine prefer food that is spicy and light in color. This food feeds the skin.

The kidneys and bladder favor food that is dark and salty. This food feeds the bones. This does not mean adding salt, but refers to food that is naturally salty.

While food also has cold and hot, yin and yang properties that are important to understand and balance, many macrobiotic diets are incomplete because they balance food only according to yin and yang and do not include the theory of the Five Phases of Energy. (More on this can be found in *Taoist Cosmic Healing*.)

When you balance your food intake, the organs are balanced and can function more efficiently. If one organ is not properly nourished, then the other organs can easily be unbalanced, becoming weak and eventually failing completely.

Before each meal, take a moment to look at the colors of the food on your plate and notice if there is something missing, or if your meal will satisfy each organ's desire.

TRUE BREATH:
FEEDING THE BODY THROUGH THE SKIN

Our existence depends on the physical food we eat and the unique combination of forces that surround us. The daily requirement of calories is about six thousand units. While we get only two thousand calories from our food, the other four thousand come from the forces surrounding us—above, below, and all around. These forces include electricity, magnetism, cosmic particle energy, light, sound, and heat. If we don't know how to absorb and transform this subtle cosmic food, we end up depending on others to provide it for us. If we do not practice our meditation, we need to ask the priests, monks, and holy men and women to give us our daily spiritual food.

The ancient Taoists discovered that we can learn to absorb the universal energies—our daily spiritual food—through the skin and the major energy centers (fig. 5.5). Absorbing energy through the skin is called the True Breath. To feel this powerful energetic technique requires a real inner smile and relaxation. The more we can relax, the more the body and the skin can open to the energy around us. The practice allows us to extend the mind to touch the force, and to draw that energy back into the body.

Fig. 5.5. Daily
spiritual food

THE RELATIONSHIP BETWEEN CHI NEI TSANG AND WISDOM CHI KUNG

Chi Nei Tsang means massage of the second brain. When I first read the *New York Times* article about the second brain research, I realized that the Taoists had been teaching the benefits of releasing the tension in the second brain through Chi Nei Tsang. I learned this massage from my master—and all he did was massage the abdominal area, working into painful areas and relaxing them (fig. 5.6). He always told me that emotions are held in the organs, and that people hold so many emotions and never release them. All kinds of emotions, like anger, frustration, hatred, fear, and jealousy get stuck inside and are held in the organs. Unless you release them and relieve this stuck condition, the organs get jammed and the nerves become tangled, obstructing the flow of energy from the second brain in the abdominal area.

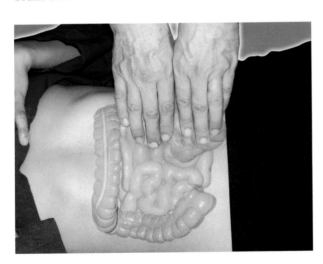

Fig. 5.6. Chi Nei Tsang: massage of the second brain

The solar plexus retains a lot of energy. It can be so hot that you cannot think, and the functioning of the second brain is completely stopped. There are so many things caught in the upper and lower abdominal area that everything clogs up and the blood cannot flow. Sometimes I see people who are so jammed up that I must tell them:

if they do not free that up, eventually it is just going to explode. Sometimes the emotions explode, sometimes the physical symptoms explode; either of these can lead to people becoming completely incapacitated. If the emotions held in the abdominal brain are released, many diseases can be cured (fig. 5.7).

Fig. 5.7. Emotions and diseases can be
released with Chi Nei Tsang.

When I was working in America, friends and students often sent people to me who were considering suicide. When people are suicidal, their abdominal area is completely hard and blocked. The troubled emotional energy is stored and held in the organs, and especially in the second brain, in the abdominal area. Since the second brain is so jammed, the head brain cannot communicate with it, and therefore essentially concludes that there is nothing going on in the abdominal brain. So the head brain gets the idea that the abdominal brain is already dead. When we start massaging the abdominal area, it is as hard as a rock. When, through massage, we soften the abdominal area, the suicidal thoughts stop. I have seen numerous cases like this.

Many serious things can happen when the abdominal brain is clogged up with emotions held in the organs.

When someone shouts at you or you see something dangerous, at times it feels just like someone has punched you in the stomach or stabbed you in the gut. Something negative happens, and the feeling is just held there in the abdomen. In today's society, we are bombarded with so much negativity and so much input from the media, and from everywhere in the crowded, frantic, polluted environment. This is compounded by the food we eat and the chemicals we put in that food, all of which add to the toxins, physical and emotional, that the gut brain has to deal with when all of what we are ingesting is completely unnatural (fig. 5.8).

Fig. 5.8. The abdomen can become compounded with negative influences.

Sometimes, when I travel, it seems that the time change, the environmental change, and all the adjustments are too much for my abdominal brain, and the whole digestive process gets jammed up. At those times, I always think about all the Chi Nei Tsang students I have, and how lucky I am to have their help. Sometimes this technique is just what it takes to get everything moving again.

Practice Abdominal Massage

Abdominal massage is something that every one of us can learn to do on and for ourselves (fig. 5.9). Try it out. In the morning, while you are lying on your bed, just put your fingers around the navel, pressing down, spiraling. You will feel much tension and tangling in the abdomen. The more pain and tension you find and then untangle, the more you will prevent any future problems. If you cannot press down on the stomach because it is so tight, this is a very dangerous condition. The entire digestive process is restricted, and the free flow of healing emotions cannot take place. In this case, it is essential that you continue to practice a gentle massage until the abdomen softens.

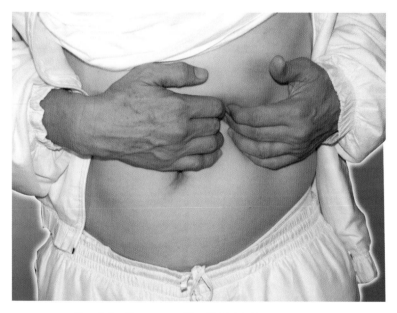

Fig. 5.9. Give yourself a Chi Nei Tsang session.

Try out the practice for at least six months. Make a commitment to this length of time, long enough to tell whether it is of benefit to you. The most important thing is to learn to hold the energy. In the beginning, you may only be able to retain the energy for ten or fifteen minutes. After a few months practice, you will find that this energy stays with you for hours, and eventually for the entire day, bringing a whole new level of alertness, focus, and concentration.

When you are not using your brain, turn it off by smiling. This turns into awareness in the tan tien or abdominal areas. As your gut brain softens and becomes more active, you can do more of the work of the head brain, which takes 80 percent of your energy, with the abdominal brain, which takes 20 percent. This is a great energy saver. Ask yourself: Which is the brain you want to use for a particular purpose? Where do you want to spend your energy? Using the head brain to do all the work is a very expensive solution.

While you are listening to someone, try smiling to the abdomen, and you just might find that you can connect very closely and more intuitively. You can become wiser and may find it easier to know what truth there is for you in what the other person is saying.

Clearing the Spirit to Increase Wisdom

As we have discussed, the brain can spend up to five times more energy than the rest of the body. Even when we are not working or consciously thinking hard, our monkey mind still wanders around, worrying, fantasizing, or daydreaming, spending the brain's energy. If we can stop the mind for a while, we can get a closer look at what exists in the body, in the organs—the strengths and weaknesses that persist inside, what needs healing. If you empty all the energy from the brain down to the organs, there will be a lot of energy returning back to be used in the brain at a later time.

When the brain is empty, and the kidney fire gets activated, you will feel the energy starting to charge the spine and the brain. When you start to activate the sexual energy, more energy can be charged to the brain and you can feel the chi pressure in the brain expand to the universe, then draw it back from the universe to fill the brain. There is an unlimited flow of energy in the universe, and it can always be accessed in times of need. When you feel too much energy, just smile to the organs, your internal universe and the excess energy will go to the tan tien.

The Wisdom practices will increase your brain capacity. When doing the practices in this chapter, the Hui Yin (yang in the yin) at the perineum has light; it is the sight or vision of the Kan (in the Kan and Li). When closing the eyes, look to the third eye and see the dot of light. This is the Li Kua, the yang within the yin. The Kan and Li, when they come together, create the Kan and Li intercourse.

When turning on the light internally the organ will exercise this light and the automatic movement of Kan and Li will start. Slowly condense the light, and the yang spirit can exit.

To improve memory, practice remembering and recalling the spirit. This can increase your memory and clear your spiritual energy from the past into the present.

RECALLING THE PAST, REWIRING BRAIN CELLS

When you practice recalling, correcting, and improving yourself, you are exercising the brain cells, and in that process you can rewire the circuits and synapses to other brain cells, clearing out unwanted memories and correcting your mistakes and inappropriate patterns (fig. 6.1).

Fig. 6.1. Clear the mind of unwanted patterns.

Passive Period

When you start to calm down the mind and the heart, old memories of hurts, wounds, abuse, and illusions from your childhood or youth may arise. Do not be afraid to let these come out. When a scenario from the past arises, watch it like you watch TV (fig. 6.2). Then let it pass. If you fully go through the past, not avoiding any of it, then the next time you sit down to practice the past will not arise. This passive period will pass by and you will no longer experience the traumas of your past.

Fig. 6.2. Watch memories arise as if watching TV.

Active Period

Recall: In sequence, recall the events of some particular occasion or period of time. For example, you can recall all the things that happened today, starting with getting up, brushing your teeth, exercising, eating breakfast, and so on, right through to the present moment, at night, when you sit down to do the meditation (fig. 6.3).

Good memories
or
Bad memories

Fig. 6.3. Recalling clears the mind of
associations of "good" and "bad" memories.

Repeat, correct, improve: As you recall the events, you can start to see which of your actions are good for you. As you continue recalling, see which ones are not good for you and resolve in the future not to repeat these patterns. Record what you learn and the corrections you want to make.

Recall the event again: Run through the sequence again. If there are other things just ahead that you must go through, see clearly what they are, and record them. See what you can reduce and simplify in your life.

Increase the brain's capacity: Use the sexual practices, such as Testicle and Ovarian Breathing, to bring the cool sexual energy up to the brain to increase the brain's capacity, knowledge, and wisdom.

This practice will improve your memory, because to recall the course of past events, you need to follow the time sequence step by step. Practice recalling to see clearly the good and bad, what is needed and what is unnecessary. Develop the power to determine the nature of the memory; and when it is finished, let go of it. Write down whatever you feel is not yet finished or corrected, and get to it the next time you do this recalling. This will increase the presence of wisdom and knowledge and help you to finish the work that should have been done on that day, thereby reducing the pressure on the psychological mind. Practice to experience feeling no pressure.

WISDOM OF THE SPIRIT

Judging and Determining: Recognition of the True and False

Learn to look inside with your inner awareness as if looking at your own spine and organs (fig. 6.4). Look and carefully determine the

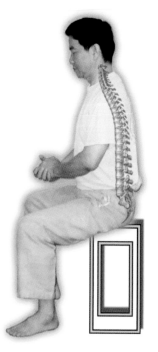

Fig. 6.4. Cultivate inner awareness by looking with your own eyes at your spinal cord and the health of your organs.

form and the shape, the size and the color of what you see. Look carefully, and determine what is false and what is true. Determine whether what you see is your own spinal cord and organs. As you continue to go deeper, investigate whether you are using your own eyes to look, or if not, what you are using to look with. With your judgment, make the determination.

When the Wisdom Chi Kung practice develops to an advanced level, automatic hand gestures (mudras) may occur, where the hand will move to the sick part and the practitioner will know the cause of the illness; a new insight may come in the form of an image.

Clear Mind

Stand firm and determined.

Practice writing: come up with a subject worth exploring, and stick with it. You can choose something that concerns a problem you have long wanted to solve, or the core issue in the healing of a disease, or your attempts in bringing healing to another person.

Decide, be firm, and determine whether your effort is okay. If you need to know the details of the subject, record the person's name, age, birth date, sex, the yin and yang, and any other pertinent information. Record this information and use it to access what is important. Write, record, and release.

If you have your own problem or sickness that needs clarification, you should not obsess on the issue, but rather, look at it in a different light. Step out of your own environment and look at it in the third person, as if you are watching TV. Choose to write on this subject, and get a new perspective.

Connection

The third eye, or Heavenly Eye, is in the center of the forehead and brain. The third eye connects to the North Star, the left eye connects to the sun, and the right eye connects to the moon. The sun and the moon move and revolve around the North Star (fig. 6.5).

The Heavenly Eye has a crack. Everyone has this; with some it is longer, with some shorter. The Heavenly Eye is our connection with the Heavenly Heart of the universe. If it is always open, you will live long. If it is closed, eventually you will die. Once you have opened it, it will stay open. When we are babies, the Heavenly Eye is open because the physical eyes are still somewhat closed. The baby is very sensitive to light—it can feel the light and use the third eye to see things.

Fig. 6.5. The third eye connection

To open the third eye, you must condense and gather the light. Close your physical eyes and extend the sight from the third eye out in front of you, and feel a force moving. See an image and the beginning of the light. Feel an internal pulsing (at the lower, middle, or upper tan tien); feel a reciprocal pulsing in the universe (the Heavenly

Heart). Let the light condense into the Heavenly Heart, the pulsing in the universe, then gradually bring it back and hold it in the Heavenly Eye. In summary: send out the light, gather it back, hold it, and let it expand in the brain.

Behind the physical eyes, about five centimeters inside the brain, is the Later Heaven Mirror. This is located between the small brain and the midbrain, in the Fourth Ventricle Room. Here, there is space that can store True Chi. The Later Heaven Mirror is tilted, and in each person the tilt of the mirror is different. The mirror is tilted just right to reflect the light downward and to connect to the two channels, the yang channel on the left and the yin channel on the right side of the spine (fig. 6.6). The Later Heaven Mirror can help people to look internally, and it has a balancing force that can help them change for the better.

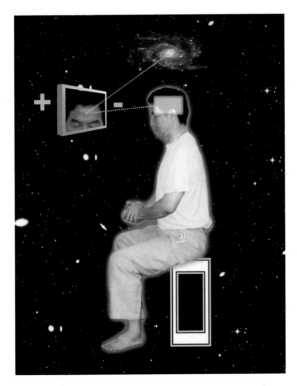

Fig. 6.6. The Later Heaven Mirror connecting to the yin and yang

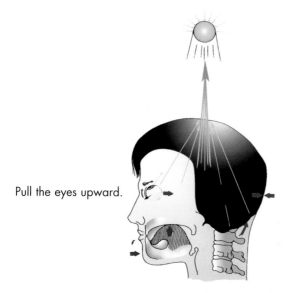

Pull the eyes upward.

Fig. 6.7. Spread a dot of light from the third eye
out into the universe.

Look out in front of your face, with eyes either open or closed, and be aware of the third eye. If you have started to see with the third eye, use the yin and yang with the Later Heaven Mirror to practice activating the force that you can feel by using the frontal bone.

In the beginning you will see one bright light, but will not be able to condense it. When you can condense the light into a dot, put the light in front of you horizontally. You can see the universe in this direction. When looking into the universe, turn the eyes upward to the back of the head. Feel the universe, and notice that the eyes can feel pain (fig. 6.7).

CULTIVATING THE SPIRIT

Here are some of the things you need to know, steps and stages you will go through in your practice, if you are serious about gaining wisdom through clearing and cultivating the spirit.

Control the Desire of the Heart

Control the heart desire and the body desire to free them from unnecessary want. Compare your body to the heavenly body, the heart (mind) as the heavens, the kidneys as the earth. Control your universe: sit quietly and picture the vast space.

Regulate the Body

Touch the tongue to the palate, close the eyes, and calm the heart. Allow the mind to be free of thought; see nothing, hear nothing, either inside or outside. Let it be natural.

Before practicing, loosen all body parts, relax the muscles, release the tension, and start the practice from this point of relaxation. Keeping the spine straight, relax and sink the chest, close the eyes, and relax the third eye.

Regulate the Breath

To regulate the breath, you first have to calm the spirit, calm the heart, and regulate the heartbeat. The heart is the seat of the spirit, and when there is no thought and no worry, it will affect the heart positively. When you can sit down and calm the heart, this is the first step to regulating the breath.

Inner Laughter and the Inner Smile

Use the three different laughing methods that you have learned (see chapter 4): laugh out loud and vibrate the stomach; laugh inside and vibrate the abdominal brain; laugh deep inside with no sound.

Gather the Sight Inward and Listen Inward

The mind and the thoughts are connected to the eyes, and sight affects the heart. Human eyes see all things and all events. To control the mind and the thoughts, we have to turn the eyes upward to look inward and listen inward.

Gather the light for the eyesight from the outside world. Look into the pores and the hair on the skin. These are the biggest energy centers of our internal universe. We have about eighty-four thousand hair follicles, and they are always connected to nature and the universe. With the exchange of the yin and yang through the Later Heaven Mirror, we transform the Former Heaven Chi into the chi in our body. Breathe this chi in through the skin. This is skin breathing: when inhaling, gather nature and the universe into your internal universe. When exhaling, radiate outward to the outer universe.

Calm the Spirit, Create the Spirit Chi, Gather the Spirit

When the heart is open, the tongue is a connection to the outside; the tongue is the sprout of the heart. The heart stores the spirit. When the tongue is not active in speaking, the heart will calm down, and the spirit will rise. The heart will be calm when you are touching the tongue to the palate.

When the heart is calm, chi rises and gathers the heart spirit. The heart opening also connects to the hearing. Gather the heart spirit through the ears. Listen inwardly; listen for the True Breath. When the True Breath is created, the spirit will gather and rise up.

Regulate the True Breath

When the regular breath stops, the True Breath will begin. This means that if you hold the breath for a moment, the internal breath—the True Breath—can rise. The chi will move in our universe.

When inhaling, think the breath down into the lower abdomen. Exhale, but do not send excess energy to the heart. Use the normal breath to activate the True Breath. The inner spirit will then calm down. If you listen inward and don't hear the True Breath, your ears are not hearing the heart. Focus on the kidney: it will produce life essence, the life essence turns into chi, chi turns to spirit, the spirit into void.

No Leaking

When looking inward and listening inward, the heart will not stir and will be calm, thoughts will not arise, and you will have the ability to turn the light on inwardly. Every True Breath will go to the root of your being. The original spirit will be aware of the skin breathing. The soul in the liver and the eyes will not leak out (leave the body); the soul in the lungs and the nose will not leak; the spirit will stay in the heart, and the mouth will not leak. The life essence will stay in the kidneys, and the ears will not leak. The mind will be calm and the spleen and the limbs will not leak.

The Cosmic Inner Smile: Raise Chi, Charge to the Brain

When the heart and the body are calmed down, be inwardly aware by looking and listening inward. Look at the inner universe, the root of the five elements. Smile to the bladder, kidneys, liver, heart, spleen, lungs, and back to the bladder for three circles in our own universe, the creative cycle. Rest and feel the chi rise up to the brain.

Concentrate and Turn the Light to Shine Inward

Concentrate on the skin breathing and picture the skin as a big energy center. While concentrating, the body doesn't move and the light will shine down. Listen to the True Breath and follow the breath.

Activate the Three Fires in Six Directions

The three fires refer to the fire energy contained within:

1. The lower abdomen, the tan tien fire, the Fire under the Sea. Taoists regard the lower tan tien as the Ocean of Chi, like fire under the water (fig. 6.8).
2. The Door of Life, the adrenal and kidney fire, the True Fire, the yang within yin.
3. The heart fire, the Imperial Fire. In the center of the heart there is one dot of green light, the essence of the heart, the yin within yang.

Opening these centers fills the body with energy and life force.

Fig. 6.8. Taoists regard the lower tan tien as the Ocean of Chi, like fire under the water.

🌀 Activating the Three Fires in Six Directions

1. Hold the palms down, parallel to the ground, lifting up the fingers. Project your mind down through the earth, passing through the space on the other side of the earth, and connect to the galaxy through the center of the palms, the Lao Gung point (fig. 6.9).
2. Move the arms and palms out slightly to the front of the body, palms still face down. As the arms move, expand your mind and feel the connection to the earth and the infinite space or galaxy below you.
3. Bring your mind back and become aware of the lower tan tien. Clear the mind, be aware of your palms facing the earth. At the

Fig. 6.9. Gather earth energy into the palms of your hands (Lao Gung). Project your mind through the earth into the infinite galaxy below you.

same time, gently pull the hands and arms back toward the body. As the arms move back, feel the chi flowing through your body and condensing into the lower tan tien. Continue to push out, touching the force and pulling it back to the body (fig. 6.10). Do this 6 to 9 times, expanding your mind, and gathering chi from the infinite space into the lower tan tien.

Fig. 6.10. Touch the force and pull it back into the lower tan tien.

4. Lift your arms and face the palms toward the lower tan tien. Feel as if you are holding a huge chi ball on the lower tan tien (fig. 6.11). Feel the fire burning under the ocean. Feel the connection between the fire in the lower tan tien and the fire energy in the universe. Feel the warmth spread through the entire body.

5. Expand your awareness to the infinite space or the galaxy behind you. Move your hands to the back and hold a huge chi fireball on the Door of Life (Ming Men). Picture two fire balls burning under the ocean. The fire will gradually burn up to the brain, to charge the brain. Within yin there is yang, stored in the kidneys and adrenal glands (fig. 6.12).

Fig. 6.11. Hold a huge ball of chi over the tan tien.

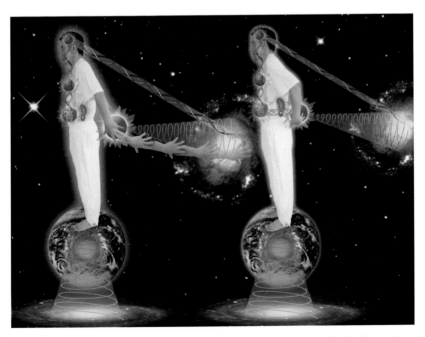

Fig. 6.12. Expand your awareness behind you, picture two fireballs under
the ocean, and draw this chi into your kidneys and adrenals.

6. Feel the chi ball pulsing and breathing, drawing energy into the body from the infinite space behind you.

7. Lift the hands, palms up, to the sides of the body and under the armpits. Feel the fingers and chi from the fingers extending into your chest, igniting the fire in the heart center, the storehouse of the original spirit (fig. 6.13).

8. Allow the heart center to open, pulsing and breathing with chi. Picture, in the middle of the heart center, a dot of green and yellow light. Within yang there is yin, inside the Imperial Fire.

9. Feel all three fires activated and resonating together—the lower tan tien, the Door of Life, and the heart center (fig. 6.14). Once you have made the connection with the forces of energy in the universe, you will learn how to store this energy in the body (fig. 6.15).

Fig. 6.13. Lift your palms to the sides of your body, fingers igniting the Imperial Fire.

Fig. 6.14. Feel all three fires resonating together.

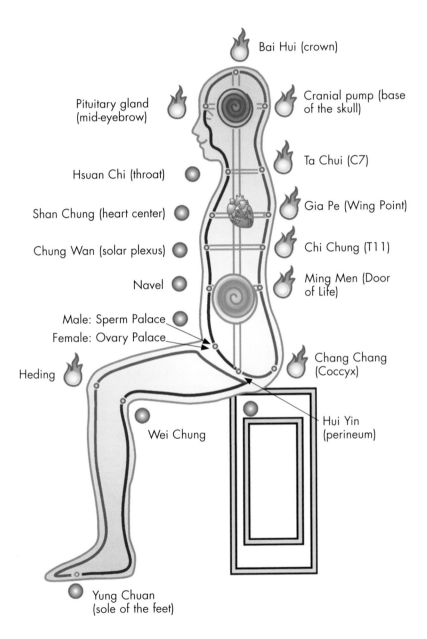

Fig. 6.15. The Microcosmic Orbit, with ancient Chinese points

REALIZING WISDOM THROUGH TRUE LIGHT: KAN AND LI IN COMBINATION

Practice until the Hui Yin has light, which is the yang within the yin. This light is the vision of the Kan. When the eyes are closed, the light you see is the yin looking out and seeing a dot of light. That is the yang within the yin, the Li Kua. The dot of light of the Li Kua in front of you is the intercourse of Kan and Li.

When you have made the connection with the forces in the universe, you want to be able to store this energy. Energy is like money: if you are making a million dollars a year and spending a million dollars, you have nothing left to use in the future. That is the way we live and use energy in our society. We are actually spending more energy than we are saving, and we are living on borrowed energy, paying very heavy interest. Our credit will run out very soon.

In the Tao practice, we store energy in the three tan tiens. The tan tiens are the reservoirs of energy within the body. These reservoirs are places where we can collect, store, and transform energy, and they are the source of energy that flows through the body. The meridians are rivers of energy that are fed by these reservoirs. The goal of opening the three tan tiens is to continually fill and replenish the meridian energy of the three tan tiens.

1. The lower tan tien in the lower abdomen, at the navel and below the navel, is like an ocean. We want to have the sense of an ocean of energy in the lower tan tien. Within this ocean, there is a fire, like a volcano under the ocean.

2. The heart center tan tien, between the two nipples, is the middle tan tien, and is associated with the fire element. Yet, within fire there is always water. The original spirit (Shen) is stored here.

3. The upper tan tien is in the brain (the Crystal Room, the Third Ventricle), and when it is full of energy, the capacity of the brain increases. Here we store our spiritual intelligence, the mind.

All the tan tiens have both yin and yang within them. In nature, the yin and yang are present in all things. Day (yang) turns into the sunset, which turns into night (yin). It is very important to feel the qualities of yin within yang and yang within yin. One quality does not exist without the other, as they are inseparable qualities of the same force.

 ## Opening the Mid-Eyebrow

1. Slowly move your palms, face up, toward both sides of the body, and slowly turn the palms toward the face. Let the middle finger be like a chi hook pointed toward the mid-eyebrow. Project your mind into space, picture the sky opening and the mid-eyebrow opening at the same time as the hand and the fingers pull to each side. Light shines into the brain, into the Third Ventricle Room (fig. 6.16). Do this 3 to 6 times.

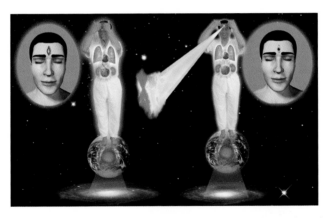

Fig. 6.16. With middle finger as a "chi hook," open the mid-eyebrow to the universe and allow light into the Third Ventricle Room.

2. Gradually let the palms face out and feel them begin to extend to touch space and connect to the galaxy. Gradually, move your palms toward the sides, and feel your palms moving and extending to the horizon, connecting to the chi in the universe. Feel them touching the left and right horizon and scooping up the whole universal chi.

3. Lift the palms up above the crown facing toward the sky. Expand your mind, sending out love and compassion, connecting with the universe or galaxy above you. Use your mind and chi together to give the universal energy a pattern, to grow and to encircle the force down into your own chi field. This enables the energy of the universe to become your own energy. Scoop up a huge chi ball, turning the palms over to face the top of the head, and pour the chi from the universe down onto the crown.

4. Picture yourself like an empty vessel, filling up with the chi from the infinite space above you. Press your tongue to the palate, and lightly squeeze the perineum (prostate gland or vagina, and anus), closing the sexual center so the universal chi will not leak out (fig. 6.17).

Fig. 6.17. Picture yourself as an empty vessel filling up with chi, and closing the sexual center so the chi does not leak out.

5. Concentrate on the soles of the feet, and feel the tingling and numbness from the crown flow down through the body. Don't hold your mind in one place for too long, because this will cause congestion and overheating. Chi needs to circulate, so all the cells of the

body can absorb the energy from the universe. If there is congestion, let go of the excess by allowing any extra energy to flow out
through the soles of the feet down to the earth (fig. 6.18).

6. Feel the chi opening the upper tan tien in the center of the head
(the Crystal Palace, the Third Ventricle) (fig. 6.19).

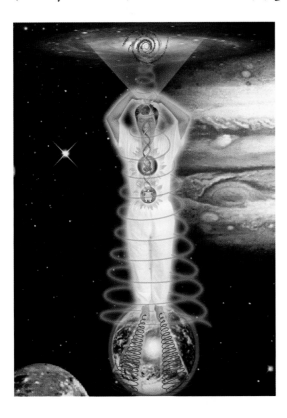

Fig. 6.18. Allow
the chi to circulate
and any excess chi
to flow through the
soles of the feet into
the earth.

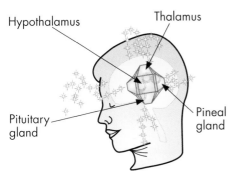

Fig. 6.19. Feel the chi opening the upper tan tien in the center of the head.

7. Draw the hands back to the point behind the heart (T5) and feel the chi extend into the heart center (fig. 6.20).

8. Gently move the hands to the T11 point behind the solar plexus. Feel the chi penetrate from the back into the solar plexus on the front (fig. 6.21).

9. Move the hands down to the Door of Life, the point opposite the navel, and feel the chi opening in the navel center.

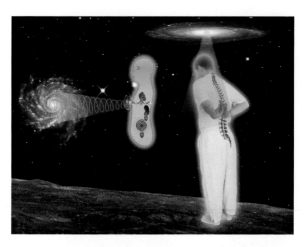

Fig. 6.20. Move the hands to the point behind the heart (T5) and feel the chi extend into the heart center.

Fig. 6.21. Feel the chi penetrate from the back into the solar plexus on the front.

10. Bring the hands to the sacrum and feel the energy penetrating to the sexual organs.
11. Bring your hands to the front of the body on top of the thighs. Glide the hands down the thighs, past the knees, and across the shins. While you glide the hands down, sink the hips and bring the tailbone down to the heels in a squatting position.
12. Feel yourself sinking through the earth and into the infinite space beyond the earth (fig. 6.22).
13. With your hands resting on your feet, lift up on the tailbone until the legs are straight. Feel the earth draw the chi from outer space into your body (fig. 6.23).

Fig. 6.22. Feel yourself sinking into infinite Earth.

Fig. 6.23. With your hands resting on the feet, lift up on the tailbone until the legs are straight.

Fig. 6.24. Slowly bring the hands to the navel and
collect the energy.

14. Squat down again, and gather more earth energy.
15. Slowly stand up, gliding the hands over the backs of the legs to the
    sacrum. Feel the chi pour into the sacrum and lower back.
16. Bring the hands to the Door of Life. Feel the chi energize the
    kidneys and Door of Life.
17. Slowly bring the hands to the navel and collect the energy
    (fig. 6.24).

 ## Cosmic Connection to the Six Directions

The goal of opening the three tan tiens is to connect ourselves to the
forces and energies in the six directions. We want to extend our minds
to connect with the infinite space and energy around us. Channeling

the six directions allows us to extend beyond this body and mind to tap into our source of energy, the Tao.

1. Press the palms down, parallel to the earth (fig. 6.25).
2. Feel the connection from the earth through the palms and into the lower tan tien.
3. Extend your chi to connect with the forces below you.
4. Lift the hands to the sides level with the ears.

Fig. 6.25. Press the palms toward the earth, connect with the tan tien, then lift the palms up level with the ears.

5. Press the palms out to both the left and the right sides, simultaneously.
6. While inhaling, connect with the horizon from the left and right sides of the body.

7. Draw the forces in from the infinite space. Focus on the lower tan tien, not the palms. This allows the energy to be absorbed into the body.
8. Bring the hands in front of the mid-eye, palms facing out. Press the palms out and connect to the infinite space in front of you.
9. Draw the hands back and bring the energy from the infinite space into the lower tan tien.
10. Lift the hands above the head, palms face down. Connect to the infinite space and universal energy above your crown.
11. Pour the chi from above into the crown. Keep your mind on the soles of your feet and feel the energy pour through all the cells.

Note: At this point you can repeat the steps for opening the three tan tiens from the previous practice:

12. Bring the hands to the navel (lower tan tien).
13. Gradually move the hands from the lower tan tien to the thighs. Feel the chi penetrate into the thighs all the way into the bone marrow.
14. Glide the hands down the thighs, past the knees, and across the shins. While you glide the hands down, sink the hips and bring the tailbone down to the heels in a squatting position.
15. Feel yourself sinking through the earth and into the infinite space beyond the earth.
16. With your hands resting on your feet, lift up on the tailbone until the legs are straight. Feel the chi drawn into your body from the earth.
17. Squat down again, and gather more earth energy.
18. Slowly stand up, gliding the hands over the backs of the legs to the sacrum. Feel the chi pour into the sacrum and lower back.
19. Bring the hands to the Door of Life. Feel the chi energize the kidneys and Door of Life.
20. Slowly bring the hands to the navel and collect the energy. Control the breath and emotions, and the sexual energy.

AWARENESS LIKE RADAR

In the various religious meditations, practitioners send consciousness and awareness out, they rest the brain, and they lower the brain waves but do not recharge the brain. There is a time and a place for this form of meditation and clearing of the mind. In the Taoist forms of meditation, we send energy out and the energy comes back into the brain, recharging it and increasing the abilities and functions of the entire brain mass. By emptying the mind down to the tan tien, we increase the energy. After Wisdom Chi Kung practice, the energy continues to increase in the brain.

My master told me that the upper brain cannot hold or store energy but can generate it well, and that the vital organs cannot generate energy but can store it well. The sexual organs produce energy the quickest, but they have to get rid of it immediately or it overheats. So if we can rest the upper brain (empty the mind down to the second mind in the tan tien), we can transform the energy into healing energy and send it up the spine to the upper brain, to heal, balance, and repair the entire system. This is Wisdom Chi Kung. We call it so because the upper mind becomes healthier and more relaxed, more balanced, so you can see and think more clearly.

All you need to do is to smile down and touch the navel, and the energy goes down to the lower brain, which rests the upper brain and creates warmth. Then, energy moves back up the spine into the third brain in the heart, while continuing to keep awareness at the navel and keep the lower tan tien warm. Thus we have three minds active: the conscious mind at the heart; the observation (or senses) mind opening up the crown; and the awareness mind at the navel, which is aware of things we were never conscious or aware of before.

To understand, consider these examples: In the "Desert Storm" war, soldiers watched underground television monitors that were connected to radar devices above ground and able to monitor a plane flying five hundred miles away. Our consciousness is like the television monitor and our awareness is like the radar device. We can also compare this consciousness, observation, and awareness to the way we can see the universe and the stars in the galaxies, without seeing them directly, using a telescope. We lower the mind down, we visualize into actualization, we use all the available energy to activate three minds focused into one mind that expands our awareness out into the universe.

Eating the Cosmos

The Taoists know saliva as the fountain of life. Saliva has a role in digestion, electrolyte balance, control of oral microflora, tissue maintenance, enamel maturation, acid neutralization, and behavior. When the saliva tastes sweet, it contains the longevity hormone; it also moisturizes the organs, the intestinal tract, and the walls of tissues, and lubricates the joints of the entire body.

When we gather and chew the saliva before swallowing it, we mix in both oxygen and the cosmic forces. Practice eating the cosmos and you will increase the fountain of life.

1. Use the tongue to sweep around the mouth and gather the saliva. When you have gathered a mouthful of nectar by moving your tongue around, mix it well like you are chewing and eating a delicious food, and eat the cosmos. We take in the cosmic particles by chewing the saliva and the sweet nectar from the brain and mixing it in the mouth.
2. Relax the mind down and let the energy move down into the earth. You are letting go of the tension, anxiety, and sick energy and sending it into the ground. Inhale, exhale, and hold. Roll the stomach while inhaling and gathering air, then exhale with a sssss sound. Chew and swallow the saliva down (fig. 6.26).
3. Inhale. Exhale and tighten the neck down.
4. Push the saliva down, forcing it through the esophagus.

Fig. 6.26. Swallow air and mix it with the saliva. Relax, chew and swallow the saliva.

5. Hold the breath, gather more saliva, and then swallow the saliva down into the stomach for absorption into the intestines and bloodstream.

Wisdom Chi Kung Summary

Through practicing the methods described in this book you are learning an effective way to gain awareness and vitality in your body, mind, and emotions. Wisdom Chi Kung uses the Inner Smile to recharge and repair the brain, to increase brain memory, and to expand the capacity of the brain. The Wisdom Chi Kung and Inner Smile practices are built on the simplest of instructions: smile, relax, and rest the monkey mind, so the brain can be recharged. If you practice diligently, you will soon take control of your positive and negative emotional energy. You will transform the negative energy into positive, in the first brain and in the second, abdominal, brain (fig. 7.1). Always remember that two brains are better than one, and creating a connection between the two is absolutely essential.

Here is a summary of the Wisdom Chi Kung practice.

1. Smile down and empty the mind to the tan tien abdominal brain.
2. Wisdom arises from the awareness and sense of appropriateness created when the head brain and abdominal brain connect.

Fig. 7.1. Wisdom Chi Kung will transform the mind.

3. Activate the tan tien fire, the Fire under the Sea, to transform the chi.

4. Activate the True Fire, the kidney fire, always retaining awareness of the tan tien.

5. Activate the heart fire, the Imperial Fire; keep the heart soft. Feel love, joy, and happiness.

6. Smile to the kidneys. Continue to empty the mind to the tan tien and the kidneys. When we empty the mind to our organs, we gain extra energy to repair and heal the body.

7. When the kidneys are filled, transformed chi will rise up and fill the back part of the brain. Keep 95 percent of the attention at the tan tien.

8. The left and right sides of the back of the brain both fill with kidney chi.

9. Smile, relax, and empty the mind to the bladder and sexual organs.

10. The bladder and sexual organs can store and transform chi.

11. The transformed chi will rise up and fill the center part of the brain with chi.

12. Smile, relax, and empty the mind into the liver and gallbladder. Let them fill with chi.

13. Chi transformed in the liver will rise up and fill the center of the right brain.

14. Smile, relax, and empty the mind to the heart and small intestine.

15. The heart and intestine can store transformed chi. Energy transformed in the organs can charge back up to the brain when the mind is empty (fig. 7.2).

Fig. 7.2. The Inner Smile meditation transforms energy in the organs.

16. Chi transformed in the heart and small intestine will charge up and fill the front part of the center of the brain.

17. Smile, relax, and empty the mind down to the stomach, spleen, and pancreas. Keep 95 percent of the attention on the tan tien.

18. Chi transformed in the stomach, spleen, and pancreas will charge the left brain with energy.

19. Relax, smile, and empty the mind down to the lungs and large intestine.

20. With an empty mind, allow the chi to transform in the lungs and large intestine.

21. Transformed chi from the lungs and large intestine rises up to fill the front part of the left and right brain.

22. Continue to empty the mind down to the tan tien and the organs. When the mind is empty, then it can be filled with transformed energy.

23. When you have emptied the mind, the transformed energy from all the organs will charge the brain with chi. Use the Inner Smile to charge energy back up to the brain to increase memory and to repair and expand the capacity of the brain.

24. With the brain filled with chi, be aware of a star of light above you. Always maintain awareness of the tan tien.

25. Be aware of the universe, with the stars and the galaxies in it. Smile and empty the mind to the universe. Relax, let go, and be completely empty.

26. Touch and be aware of the universe, of the stars and the galaxies in it. Continue to be aware of the tan tien, so you do not lose yourself.

27. Open yourself to contain the universe. Combine all universal energies with the transformed chi at the tan tien. This is the secret of all the great masters.

28. Combine your chi and good intention with the high universal energy, and let this multiply while you retain a majority of your awareness at the tan tien.

Fig. 7.3. The Wisdom Chi Kung practice fills the brain and the whole body with transformed energy.

29. Then the energy will return to you multiplied many times to fill the brain and the whole body (fig. 7.3).
30. Hold the enhanced chi in the brain for as long as it is comfortable. As your practice deepens, you will be able to hold it longer.
31. Empty the mind down to the tan tien once again. Feel this enhanced energy fill the tan tien with a higher frequency of chi, which will be further refined and enhanced in the tan tien and available to fill the brain again.
32. Once the brain has been filled again, empty the mind again to the universe. When it is empty, the mind can then be filled with higher life force, which will open the capacity for increased understanding and wisdom.

Combine chi and good intention with the universal energy, and it will be returned to you, multiplied many times, to fill you with enhanced life force (fig. 7.4).

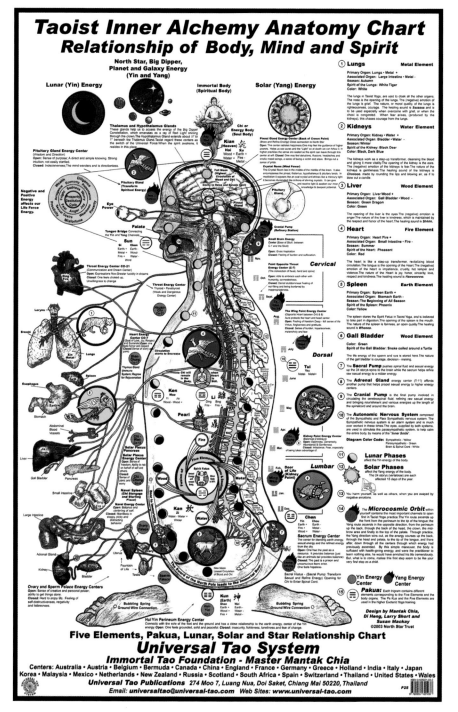

Fig. 7.4. Body, mind, and soul filled with life force

Appendix
Questions and Answers about the Wisdom Chi Kung Practice

Q. What is the Taoist belief on generating life-force energy?

A. First the sexual organs: The Taoists discovered that although the sexual organs are responsible for *generating* a lot of sexual energy (life force), they cannot *store* the energy efficiently. Once a certain amount of energy has been generated, some energy has to be dumped out. This is a loss of the best energy available. The sexual organs are actually very efficient at storing energy *before* it has been "generated" or brought into manifestation. That is why the sexual energy is so powerful.

The brain can access and generate the higher forces, but it cannot store this energy in the brain. We need to train the brain to increase its ability and its capacity to store energy. The brain's energy, when increased to a certain level, can enable more synapses to grow, and can help convert protein into material the brain cells can use. Taoists believe that with training and practice, one can learn to grow more brain and nerve cells, as well as increase the number of synapses or connections between the nerve cells in the central nervous system and higher forces.

The organs of the body can also generate energy, but much less than the sexual organs and the brain. They do, however, have a much greater capacity to store and transform energy.

The three tan tiens also can store energy, as well as transform and supply it to the brain, spinal cord, sexual organs, and other organs. Most Taoist sources say that the tan tiens do not even have a physical location and that they are not to be looked for in any place.

The aim of Taoist basic training is to integrate the brain, sexual organs, and internal organs into one system. If the brain generates an excess of energy, this energy can be stored in the organs. Excess sexual energy can also be stored in the organs and three tan tiens. If the brain generates a surplus of "higher forces" and we are unable to store this energy, we end up having to throw it away. It is like preparing food for one hundred people, and only one person eating. The rest is wasted. The same is true if too much sexual energy is produced and there is no practice in how to store it. We have a limited amount of energy and cannot afford to waste it.

Q. Why are increased connections between synapses in the brain necessarily good if the point of the practice is to empty the mind?

A. Increased synapses enable the cells to make more connections with other cells, and essentially, with the cosmos. Synapses are like the spokes on a wheel: the more spokes, the more the energy can disperse its information, therefore reducing the amount of pressure built up on the wheel (cell) itself. Inside the cell is the pressure of all the essential information that the cell contains. When cells have the ability to release more information through increased synapses, the amount of traffic is reduced because the cell can communicate at a higher rate. When traffic is reduced, the thoughts become less, and the mind is released from the constant input.

Q. What is the basis of the belief that the liver, heart, and kidneys are capable of generating huge amounts of energy? If they do store emotions and energy, what kind of energy, and is this the same energy generated by the brain? Is this related to the higher forces that the brain can "access and generate"?

A. The brain is like an electromagnetic force field; it can generate and pick up this kind of energy, and continue to generate a frequency measured by the biofeedback machine. The heart is capable of generating the magnetic field of love or healing power, and this field can radiate out three meters to a thousand meters wide. The lower tan tien generates a general chi wave, measuring as infrared light like that produced from the sun. The kidney, however, acts as the storage place of sexual energy, and holds a yin essence or water energy. The kidney can balance the heart, which is a hot fire energy. The liver is a storage area for emotions and toxins, especially the emotions of anger and frustration. The liver holds a more yang essence than the kidney, but less yang than that of the heart.

Q. Why is it so important to increase the level of energy in the brain?

A. Each brain cell has synapses that connect to many other similar cells. The brain is also filled with proteins, which, under normal conditions, the brain cannot fully utilize. If we raise the level of energy in the brain, and maintain the brain in this enhanced state for a period of time, at a certain point the brain cells can grow new synapses and increase the capacity of each cell.

Q. What do you mean by "raise the level of energy"?

A. Every day we use up so much of our brain's capacity to function, that by the end of the day we have very little energy left to do anything. When we smile into our organs, we have the capability of charging the brain with more energy so that we increase our total brainpower.

Q. Is this the same kind of "energy" used by the body?

A. When we think or worry excessively the brain can use up to about 80 percent of the whole body's energy. This leaves only 20 percent for the rest of the organism. If we can stop the brain for a short moment, guide the brain to stop all the emotions, worry, and excess thinking, we can regain the lost brainpower. Our brainpower and concentration or focus diminishes as we grow older. It is also necessary to rest and eat the right foods to maintain energy.

Q. What are some ways to increase brainpower?

A. With these Universal Tao basic practices, each practice will raise your energy level and recharge the brain with energy. You need to practice three times a day, holding the chi in the brain and the spine. Start by activating the fire in the tan tien, opening the Microcosmic Orbit, and generating wisdom.

Q. What is the best way to generate wisdom?

A. The sexual practice is the most powerful, including the Testicle and Ovarian Breathing practice and the Power Lock. Empty the mind, and fill the internal organs and sexual organs. Many people are disconnected with this part of their body. By becoming familiar with it, you will increase the wisdom of your entire body and system.

Q. What do you mean when you say people have become disconnected?

A. Today the mind and organs have become separate functions because of the way most people in society live. Taoism believes that the mind, body, and spirit must work together in order to be connected. We must have unity within the body, mind, and spirit.

Q. What happens when one empties the mind without "using" this energy elsewhere in the body?

A. This form of meditation is useful for contacting other realms of reality, and altered states of consciousness. Measurements show that there are no brain waves, muscle tension is low, the energy in the brain is significantly reduced as the person meditating goes into a deeper and deeper state of relaxation. When the person returns to normal waking state her brain remains low in energy. She often remains in a semi-relaxed state that makes it difficult to function well in the outside world.

Q. If there are no brain waves, what exactly is meant by contacting other realms of reality?

A. Monks are also able to go into a deeply relaxed state with few brain waves and little brain activity. When chanting and praying there is an increase in the brain energy. This enables the chanter to quiet his mind with no muscle tension. He feels very tranquil and able to release attachments to this world. This energy quickly dissipates when the person stops the practice; there is only a momentary increase in energy but no lasting increase.

Q. How do you experience an "increase in brain energy" and "quieting the mind" at the same time?

A. The more energy can be charged to the brain, the more the brain can be calm. When thinking too much the brain is empty and weak, and will only continue to think and begin to worry. When the organs are full with energy, it will charge the brain, but it requires that the mind first be emptied down to the organs, and in reverse will strengthen the brain and begin to quiet the mind.

Q. Is it possible to reduce muscle tension and increase energy in the brain at the same time?

A. Master Chia was able to significantly reduce the brain-wave activity (sleeping state) and increase the amount of energy flowing to his brain while simultaneously reducing muscle tension. This showed that he was in a state of deep relaxation while his brain was filling with energy. The people testing him were able to talk and converse with Master Chia about what was happening with him while he was meditating and while he stayed in a deep state of relaxation.

Q. What was Master Chia doing to make this possible?

A. While doing the Inner Smile meditation, Master Chia would smile and bring energy to the various internal organs. The outcome was that energy in the brain increased.

Q. What happens when the brain is filled with energy after the meditation is completed?

A. While the brain's energy shows marked increase during the meditation, it also continues to hold the energy long after the meditation has ended. Furthermore, there was a continual increase in the right brain activity until the two hemispheres (left and right) were almost equal.

Bibliography

Chia, Mantak. *Chi Nei Tsang: Chi Massage for the Vital Organs.* Rochester, Vt.: Destiny Books, 2003.

———. *Healing Light of the Tao: Foundational Practices to Awaken Chi Energy.* Rochester, Vt.: Destiny Books, 2008.

———. *Bone Marrow Nei Kung: Taoist Techniques for Rejuvenating the Blood and Bone.* Rochester, Vt.: Destiny Books, 2006.

———. *Energy Balance through the Tao: Exercises for Cultivating Yin Energy.* Rochester, Vt.: Destiny Books, 2005.

———. *Taoist Cosmic Healing: Chi Kung Color Healing Principles for Detoxification and Rejuvenation.* Rochester, Vt.: Destiny Books, 2003.

———. *Golden Elixir Chi Kung.* Rochester, Vt.: Destiny Books, 2005.

———. *Cosmic Fusion: The Inner Alchemy of the Eight Forces.* Rochester, Vt.: Destiny Books, 2007.

Netter, Frank H., M.D. *Interactive Atlas of Human Anatomy*, www.netterimages.com, 1995.

Tortora, Gerard J., and Sandra Reynolds Grabowski. *Introduction to the Human Body*, 5th Ed. New York: John Wiley & Sons, 2001.

———. *Principles of Anatomy and Physiology*, 9th ed. New York: McGraw-Hill, 1999.

 About the Author

Mantak Chia has been studying the Taoist approach to life since childhood. His mastery of this ancient knowledge, enhanced by his study of other disciplines, has resulted in the development of the Universal Tao System, which is now being taught throughout the world.

Mantak Chia was born in Thailand to Chinese parents in 1944. When he was six years old, he learned from Buddhist monks how to sit and "still the mind." While in grammar school he learned traditional Thai boxing, and soon went on to acquire considerable skill in Aikido, Yoga, and Tai Chi. His studies of the Taoist way of life began in earnest when he was a student in Hong Kong, ultimately leading to his mastery of a wide variety of esoteric disciplines, with the guidance of several masters, including Master I Yun, Master Meugi, Master Cheng Yao Lun, and Master Pan Yu. To better understand the mechanisms behind healing energy, he also studied Western anatomy and medical sciences.

Master Chia has taught his system of healing and energizing practices to tens of thousands of students and trained more than two thousand instructors and practitioners throughout the world. He has established centers for Taoist study and training in many countries around the globe. In June 1990 he was honored by the International Congress of Chinese Medicine and Qi Gong (Chi Kung), which named him the Qi Gong Master of the Year.

The Universal Tao System and Training Center

THE UNIVERSAL TAO SYSTEM

The ultimate goal of Taoist practice is to transcend physical boundaries through the development of the soul and the spirit within the human. That is also the guiding principle behind the Universal Tao, a practical system of self-development that enables individuals to complete the harmonious evolution of their physical, mental, and spiritual bodies. Through a series of ancient Chinese meditative and internal energy exercises, the practitioner learns to increase physical energy, release tension, improve health, practice self-defense, and gain the ability to heal him- or herself and others. In the process of creating a solid foundation of health and well-being in the physical body, the practitioner also creates the basis for developing his or her spiritual potential by learning to tap into the natural energies of the sun, moon, earth, stars, and other environmental forces.

The Universal Tao practices are derived from ancient techniques rooted in the processes of nature. They have been gathered and integrated into a coherent, accessible system for well-being that works directly with the life force, or chi, that flows through the meridian system of the body.

Master Chia has spent years developing and perfecting techniques for teaching these traditional practices to students around the world through ongoing classes, workshops, private instruction, and healing sessions, as well as through books and video and audio products. Further information can be obtained at www.universal-tao.com.

THE UNIVERSAL TAO TRAINING CENTER

The Tao Garden Resort and Training Center in northern Thailand is the home of Master Chia and serves as the worldwide headquarters for Universal Tao activities. This integrated wellness, holistic health, and training center is situated on eighty acres surrounded by the beautiful Himalayan foothills near the historic walled city of Chiang Mai. The serene setting includes flower and herb gardens ideal for meditation, open-air pavilions for practicing Chi Kung, and a health and fitness spa.

The center offers classes year-round, as well as summer and winter retreats. It can accommodate two hundred students, and group leasing can be arranged. For information worldwide on courses, books, products, and other resources, see below.

RESOURCES

Universal Healing Tao Center
274 Moo 7, Luang Nua, Doi Saket, Chiang Mai, 50220 Thailand
Tel: (66)(53) 495-596 Fax: (66)(53) 495-852
E-mail: universaltao@universal-tao.com
Web site: www.universal-tao.com

For information on retreats and the health spa, contact:
Tao Garden Health Spa & Resort
E-mail: info@tao-garden.com, taogarden@hotmail.com
Web site: www.tao-garden.com

Good Chi • Good Heart • Good Intention

 Index

Numbers in italics indicate illustrations.

meditation
  brain waves stopped during, 7–8
  Buddhist, 5, 7–8
  Cosmic Healing Sounds, 7
  Cosmic Orbit, 7, *115*
  ending, 84–85
  Microcosmic Orbit, *115*
  with and without healing energy, *3*
  Zen, 5, 7–8
  See also Taoist meditation
memory
  improving, 44, 99, 101–2, 128
  recalling the past, 7–8, 99–101
  recorded in the heart, 37
  See also brain
meridians, 116, 139
Microcosmic Orbit, *115*
mid-eyebrow, opening, 117–22
mind
  awareness mind, 125–27
  calming, 2, 81, 138
  clear mind, 2, 103
  in deep state of relaxation, 137
  emptying down to the tan tien, *1*,
    21–22, 78, *79*
  emptying into the organs, 69, 138
  energy used by, 38–39, 40
  fusion practice for, 26–28
  monkey mind, 10, 12, 38–39, 40
  reconnecting with body and spirit,
    19–22
  See also brain
mirror, Later Heaven, 105, 106
mudras, 103
muscle tension, 30–31, 138

navel, 82, *83*, 125

nervous system, 15–16, 33
North Star, 103, 104

organs
  connecting with brain, 12–14,
    20–21, 98, 135
  emotions held in, 9, 93–94
  emptying mind into, 69, 138
  energy transformed in, 130
  five element correspondences, *48*
  food needed by, 91
  generating and storing energy in,
    20, 21–22
  illustration, *16*
  smiling down to, *13*, 14, 72–75
Orgasmic Upward Draw, 7
ovarian breathing, 101

pancreas, 91
past, recalling, 7–8, 99–101
prostate gland, 23
pumps, three, 51, 55–61

realms of reality, 137
recalling the past, 7–8, 99–101
research
  Master Chia case study, 30–33
  on Taoist meditation, 1–8
Riding the Horse, 50
right-handed people, 43–44

sacral pump, 50, 55–58
sacred dance, 57
saliva nectar, 52–53, 82, *83*, 126–27
science, Western, 1–9
second brain
  ability to think, 9, 18

BOOKS OF RELATED INTEREST

Inner Traditions • Bear & Company
P.O. Box 388
Rochester, VT 05767
1-800-246-8648
www.InnerTraditions.com

Or contact your local bookseller